ANCIENT

CIVILIZATIONS

Hill Tech Ventures Inc.
Publishing Division | Nanaimo, Canada
Printed in the United States

ANCIENT

CIVILIZATIONS

Discover the Ancient Secrets of

the Greek, Egyptian, and

Roman Civilizations

MARTIN R. PHILLIPS

ABOUT THE AUTHOR

MARTIN R. PHILLIPS

 Martin R. Phillips is an extremely passionate historian, archaeologist, and most recently a writer. Ever since Martin was a young boy he has been fascinated with ancient cultures and civilizations.

In 1990, Martin graduated with distinction from the University of Cambridge with a double major in History and Archaeology. Upon graduation, Martin worked as an archeologist and travelled the world working in various excavation sites. Over the years, while working as an archaeologist, Martin became very well cultured and gained great insights into some of the most historic civilizations to ever exist. This first hand insight into the ancient cultures of the world is what sparked Martin's newest passion, history writing and story telling.

In 2012, Martin decided to retire from archeology to focus on writing. Over the years he has seen and experienced a great deal of fascinating things from all over world. Martin now spends the majority of his free time putting all of his research, experience, and thoughts onto paper in an attempt to share his knowledge of the ancient cultures with the world.

Over the past few years Martin has excelled in his writings. His narrative style has a way of combining the cold hard facts with a story teller's intrigue which makes for an excellent reading experience.

"Live your life to the fullest and enjoy the journey!"

- Martin R. Phillips

PART 1

ANCIENT GREECE

PART 2

ANCIENT EGYPT

PART 3

ANCIENT ROME

PART 1
ANCIENT GREECE

Ancient Secrets of the Greeks

INTRODUCTION

Ancient Greece is, without a doubt, one of the most fascinating cultures that our world has ever seen! Whether you look at their mythology, their history, or their philosophy, the Ancient Greek civilization has permeated our approach to, and understanding of, the world at large. It is impossible to tell the story of modern civilization without providing some recognition to the influence of Greece.

The Greek Empire was vast, encompassing over 700 individual city-states, 150-173 of which would form the Delian League in an effort to combat the onslaught of Persia. How did so many city-states come together under one rule? With only a fraction joining the Delian League, how did these city-states *stay* together in times of disagreement and conflict?

There are hundreds, if not thousands of questions regarding this vast and fascinating civilization. One could spend years and write many volumes on each period of the Ancient Grecian culture, history, and mythology. It has been my pleasure to assemble this research, and the voice of Greece itself (through reference to its own historians, including Herodotus,

Thucydides, and Xenophon.) I am excited to share with you an admittedly brief look at the civilization we know as Ancient Greece (a full history would take more pages than the unabridged Oxford English Dictionary and the Encyclopedia Britannica combined.)

In this book you will find the history and opinions of the Ancient Greeks. You will discover their truth and their mythology. You will learn of war and peacetime. There are heroes and villains, saints and scoundrels. You will find philosophies that changed the world, and continue to do so even to this day.

For the most part, the contents of this book are arranged topically as opposed to strictly chronologically to allow specific areas of interest in the Ancient Greeks and their civilization to be more easily accessible. However, care has been taken to include the approximate dates of people and events to give you a good idea of the chronology of the content.

The importance of the Greek civilization cannot be overstated. In nearly every facet of our lives, we can find something which had its roots, or took a new turn in Ancient Greece. When you go to the polls to elect an official, you are operating on a Greek principle. When you discuss the nature of life with others, you are performing a modified version of the Greek symposium. Even when you sit down to watch television, or read a book, you often find references to Trojan wars, Sparta and their role in the conflict with the

Persians, the philosophy, or the character of the Greeks.

As you rediscover Ancient Greece, I encourage you to make note of how much of that vast and diverse civilization still lives on throughout our world today.

CHAPTER **1**

The Beginning

While the earliest portions of what would come to be ancient Greece are largely lost to antiquity, there is still quite a bit that we can deduce from the evidence that we do have.

The era commonly known as ancient Greece began in the 8th century BC and lasted until around the 7th century AD with the end of antiquity. Ancient Greece consisted of a few distinct periods of Greek government and culture. These include the Archaic, Classical, Hellenistic, and Roman periods.

This chapter, however, will give you a brief outline of the time period preceding that of what we commonly call Ancient Greece. Points of focus include: The Neolithic Era, The Bronze Age including the Minoan, Cycladic, and Mycenaean civilizations, and the Greek Dark Age.

The Neolithic Era: 6,800-3,200 BC

While there was activity in the area which would come to be known as Ancient Greece before these periods, The Neolithic era saw the stabilization of the climate, the introduction of farming, stock-rearing, and pottery; and the building of settlements among other important matters.

The last Glacial Period (inaccurately termed the last Ice Age) ended around 8,000 BC, and this led to the advent of more permanent settlements in Greece. Prior to this period, many peoples were nomadic, but with the stabilization of the climate, they were able to build these permanent settlements.

The economy was largely based on a barter system where goods and services were traded for produce from farmers, cattle and other stock, and pottery. This diversification allowed people to focus more on one particular kind of work as they could barter their trade for whatever provisions they needed.

Settlement and the meeting of an individual's daily needs (food, water, etc.) led to the advent of crafts-men. These people were specialists in their particular areas, and trade became a more important facet of everyday life. People turned to outside sources to supplement things which were either unavailable, or in short supply in their given areas, and everyone was able to meet their essential needs without the necessity of traveling from place to place. Neolithic settlements were often fortified, but allowed trade and travel for its citizens.

Although hunting and gathering provided individuals with much more free time than agriculture has, it was also much less efficient. It would take about 1,000 calories of expenditure to obtain 1,000 calories of food, thus surplus was relatively unheard of. People had to move from place to place as nomads in order to ensure that they could hunt and gather enough food to sustain them.

The Neolithic Age is often known as the last period of the Stone Age. Tools were usually made of stone, as well as weapons, building materials, and other necessities as it was extremely plentiful in all areas of the habitable world.

The advent of agriculture, often known as either the agricultural revolution or The Neolithic Revolution, allowed people to remain in one place and actually obtain a surplus of food. Having a food surplus allowed settlements to grow and, although without agriculture people had more time, less use for slave labor, very little impact on their (and subsequently) our environment, Ancient Greece, let alone modern civilization would be impossible in the way we know it.

Aegean Civilization (The Greek Bronze Age): 3,200-1,050 BC

The Aegean civilization is a reference to The Bronze Age settlements of Greece in and around the Aegean Sea. The Aegean Bronze Age started around 3,200 BC, (Aegean Islands around 3,000 BC, and Crete in about 2,800 BC,) although there is a great deal of speculation on the exact dates. Initially, bronze was very expensive, and so it was typically reserved for the wealthy. In fact, the class system of civilization was largely initiated based on the availability of these metals, and who had them.

Due to its initially limited supply, bronze took quite a while to become commonplace, but was generally in use beginning around 2,800 BC. What led to its popularity and widespread use was the fact that bronze was much easier to use than traditional tools, and thus it eventually replaced stone for tools and weapons.

In Greece, The Bronze Age was typified by the expansion of settlements, the development of navigation, the growth of individual dwellings, and further class stratification. During this time, trade became more and more vital to the growth and sustainability of cities and thus found great expansion.

There were three predominant groups in the area of Greece during this time. They were the Minoan, the Cycladic, and the Mycenaean civilizations.

The Cycladic civilization existed from approx. 3,200-2,000 BC. The Cycladic civilization was located on a number of islands in the Aegean Sea, most notably around the Cyclades. Although not much is known about the inner-workings of this civilization, we do have archaeological evidence which suggests that they were seafaring people who were notable for sculpture. Some evidence shows signs of copper-working. Their sculptures have been found in various places in the Greek area, including Knossos on the island of Crete. With the exception of Delos, this group drifted into the background with the advent of Cretan palace-culture.

Like the Cyclades, there isn't much specific knowledge of the Minoan civilization. In fact, the term Minoan was coined by Arthur Evans, and is taken from the mythical King Minos, a son of Zeus and Europa. The Minoans controlled many of the Greek Islands, most notably Crete

The Minoan Civilization on Crete lasted from approx. 2,700 BC to 1,450 BC, and began in the city of Knossos. The island was rich in natural resources, and the Minoans took great part in overseas trading. They were largely merchants and fishermen, although they made use of lumber for trading and building their sea craft. There were craftsmen, and traders, indicating a proliferation of craft specialization. The Minoan civilization of Crete was invaded by the Mycenaeans in about 1,400 BC. Their written language is known as Linear A, and is presently indecipherable.

The Mycenaeans, often referred to as "Proto-Greeks," were a Helladic (of mainland Greece) civilization from approx. 1,600-1,050 BC, although they did come to control many of the Greek Islands during the span of their civilization. They did speak an early form of Greek and had two predominant forms of written language known as Linear A and Linear B. While Linear B was largely deciphered in the 1950s, Linear A remains indecipherable. As there are no written historical accounts that we're presently aware of about the Mycenaeans *by* the Mycenaeans, historians have been able to trace their culture through by tracking their pottery.

The Mycenaeans get their name from archaeologists of the 19th century from the name of their capitol city of Mycenae, which is located about 56 miles (90 kilometers) southwest of Athens. Mycenae is also well-known for being the city from which the mythical Agamemnon ruled in Homer's Iliad. In The Iliad, the Trojan wars were fought between the peoples of Mycenae and the city of Troy. The storyline of the Greek poet Homer The Iliad beginning nine years after the beginning of the mythical Trojan War.

The Mycenaeans were bold traders, fierce warriors, and phenomenal engineers made up of numerous cities connected by a common language and culture. The people were governed by a singular king who had ultimate power to levy taxes, and generally govern the people. These kings were extremely wealthy

Mycenaean buildings were usually built atop a hill and were made of stone, both of which suggest that they were designed with defense in mind. Some of these structures are still standing today, including the Lion's Gate in Mycenae.

The economy was a palace-economy, a moneyless system where goods are stored in a central location and doled out to the people as needed. These goods were largely the products of farming and trade.

The collapse of the Mycenaean civilization occurred sometime between 1,200 and 1,050 BC. The reasons for the collapse are unknown; however the cities of this civilization were either abandoned or, in many cases, destroyed. Speculation about the collapse includes rebellion, invasion, or possibly a widespread natural disaster.

CHAPTER 2

The Pantheon of the Gods

To understand what the religion of Ancient Greece was to its people is to understand a great deal about the people themselves. These gods and goddesses along with the mythos attached to them would dominate Greek knowledge and philosophy for centuries.

The Greek Religion was polytheistic (belief in multiple gods) and these gods were said to interact with people on a constant basis. Many women would claim that they had gotten pregnant through intercourse with one of the chief deities, often Zeus himself. Others claimed that their injuries or diseases were cured by the gods' own intervention. Still more attributed military victories, social and political success, acts of nature, and various other positive and negative personal or collective experiences to the intervention of these gods.

Rather than simply provide a list of the gods and their attributions, it seems fitting to give a closer account of the chief gods and their powers, their hierarchical structure, and effects on Ancient Greek civilization. Along with the gods themselves, the religion, morality, and general mythology bear investigation.

The gods were not the omnipotent, ambivalently benevolent gods which dominate the cultural landscape today. The gods behaved and appeared much more like the people who worshipped them. The gods weren't just jealous of the others, they were also believed to engage in (consensual and nonconsensual) sexual intercourse on a regular basis, and had the same human emotions and imperfections as the people who worshipped them.

There was a power structure to the pantheon with Zeus as its king. Zeus was the youngest son of Cronus and Rhea and had a modicum of control over all of the other gods. However, many myths and legends have the other gods sneaking around behind Zeus's back and causing all sorts of mischief. Zeus controlled the weather, and wielded lightning bolts. He is said to have ruled the Olympians (in this case, the inhabitant gods of Olympus) as a father ruled his family.

Although in most traditions Zeus is married to Hera, his frequent sexual exploits resulted in his various children with other deities and, quite often, with mortal women as well as in the case of Heracles (often called Hercules.) In most instances of his intercourse with goddesses, the children were born as new gods or goddesses such as Athena, Hermes, and Ares (to name a brief few.) His affairs with mortal women, however, often resulted in beings such as Heracles who were a hybrid of hero and god.

The gods of the ancient Greeks often presided over various functions of nature, such as Helios as the god who controlled the movement of the sun; and Poseidon who ruled over the sea. Other times, the gods were behind different emotions or states of being such as Aphrodite who ruled over love; and Uranus who was the god of the sky, or the heavens.

Other notable entities included the primordial gods such as Chaos, the father of life, the universe, etc.; and Aether who was the god of the pure upper air of the Olympians (not to be confused with the normal air that mortals breathe.)

There were the Titans who were a powerful race of gods who spawned (and were subsequently overthrown by) the Olympians such as Mnemosyne who was the personification of memory and was mother to the muses; and Cronus (often Kronos) who was the father of Zeus and led the revolt against Uranus (the sky.)

Cronus is particularly of interest in Greek mythology in that he feared losing power to his children as his father had lost power to him. He therefore ate five of his six children one by one. The sixth child, Zeus, was saved by his mother (Cronus's wife and sister) Rhea when, after Zeus's birth, she presented a stone to Cronus, swaddled in cloth so that he would be unaware that he was not consuming his new son. When Zeus grew up, he forced Cronus to imbibe a potion which caused the latter to vomit up the children which he had devoured. Thus, his siblings were reborn. The siblings: Demeter, Hestia, Hera, Hades, Poseidon and Zeus joined together to wage war against their father and the rest of the Titans, eventually bound and launched into oblivion.

Other gods and godlike beings included The Muses who were said to be the goddesses of inspiration. There were Nymphs who were divine beings who animated different aspects of nature. There were the Giants, and their relatives the Cyclopes who were one-eyed giants. Along with these, there were also various beings consisting of half-humans or human-like beings such as satyrs (half-man and half-goat,) centaurs (half-man and half horse,) and gorgons (hideous female creatures with hair made of live, venomous snakes,) of which Medusa is a well-known example.

Many books could be and have been written about the various gods, titans, etc. What is important is how the belief in these gods affected the Greeks in their culture and in their daily lives.

Greek morality was largely based on striving toward moderation, as most vices were considered acceptable in-and-of themselves, while taking these things to extremes, such as overeating, excessive drinking, etc. would lead one to great error.

Hubris (extreme pride to the point of delusion) was the most feared and despised of vices, as it was seen as a chief cause behind things such as rape, murder, and betrayal. Pride itself wasn't considered a negative thing, however when it reached the point of hubris, it had reached the point of being out of control, and was often personified as pridefulness and an overestimation of one's abilities to the exclusion of others' rights.

Many of the Greek city-states were based upon a belief that a particular deity was the city's patron. Who the people chose as their city-state's patron shows a lot about the focus of that city-state. Athens for instance was named for their patron goddess Athena. The city was therefore primarily concerned with education and knowledge, as Athena was the goddess of wisdom. Sparta had two: Ares, and Artemis. Ares, the god of war signified Sparta's focus on military might while Artemis, the god of the hunt among other things.

Many of the Greek myths were used to explain natural phenomena. One such myth is that of Persephone and Hades. It was said that Persephone, the unspeakably gorgeous daughter of Demeter, goddess of fertility, was working in a field one day when the earth cracked open, and she was taken to the underworld by Hades. For nine days, Demeter searched for her daughter, neglecting the crops of the earth which caused them to die off. Zeus, seeing that humanity could not survive without Demeter to make the earth fertile again, intervened, and demanded that Hades release Persephone to be with her mother. Hades agreed to release Persephone so long as she hadn't eaten anything while in the underworld. However, Hades had tricked Persephone into eating pomegranate seeds. It was finally decided that while Persephone would be allowed to live with her mother during most of the year, she would have to return to Hades for three months. During the time in which Persephone was with her mother, crops flourished; however during her three months with Hades, the world became cold and barren. Such was the explanation for winter.

The Olympic Games were originally established to pay tribute to Zeus. Along with these games, which were held in the city of Olympia, animals were sacrificed to Zeus. Priests would then take the blood of the slaughtered animals and spread it on an altar in the temple of Zeus to further honor their deity.

One more tradition in Greek religion was the development of mystery schools. These schools or cults were each dedicated to a particular deity. For instance, the Eleusinian mystery school was a cult of Demeter. Anyone who had clean hands, in other words had not committed a blood offense such as murder, was allowed entry; however communication with anyone outside who was uninitiated was strictly forbidden. An example of how serious this secrecy was occurred when two teenage boys were caught spying on the rites of the Eleusinian cult. The punishment for those boys was death.

CHAPTER 3

The Birth of Democracy

Moving from mythology back to historical fact, we come to the Athenian Revolution in 508 BC. The people, who had been oppressed for hundreds of years by those in power, revolted against their rulers. The people would find the solution to their trials in one of the most unlikely people.

There are two common approaches to the Athenian Revolution, and both will be taken here in the interest of covering the topic as thoroughly as possible, as this conflict and its resulting governmental changes would change the way that Greece, and subsequently the world, would approach politics. One is to focus on Cleisthenes himself, the other is to look more at the character of the people who fought for their freedom.

Cleisthenes, born around 570 BC, was an aristocrat who, like others of his ilk, had been brought up to be a ruler. He was a descendant of Cleisthenes of Sicyon, a tyrant. The term tyrant in those days didn't necessarily denote corruption; rather it described an absolute ruler. Cleisthenes was born and brought up in a palatial home, and was reared with the belief that certain privileges were his by right of his noble birth.

The political climate of Greece during this time period was largely a struggle between city-states to gain land or influence from another. Oftentimes a polis (city-state) would be struggling for its independence from another. Although many aspects of the Greek city-states were shared, such as the overall religion, there was no common system of governance, and each polis was under its own ruler(s).

Athens in the early days of Cleisthenes, as well as during the Athenian revolution was a relatively small polis which was led by an individual tyrant. The tyrant whose corruption led the Athenians to their historical revolt was Hippias, son of Peisistratus (Cleisthenes's brother-in-law.)

Peisistratus came to power in Athens by having an especially tall girl from a neighboring village accompany him to Athens. He claimed that she was Athena herself, and demanded that he be given rule of the polis. The people welcomed him as their ruler. Peisistratus, in order to ensure his continued power over the polis of Athens, appealed to the common people. He offered the people prosperity by lowering taxes and doling out free loans, not only to ensure that the people were in his favor, but also to build up the polis itself.

Under the rule of Peisistratus, Athens was transformed from a smaller rural polis into a center of trade and innovation. The rule of Peisistratus was a great departure from the aristocracy which had dominated Athens and, indeed, most of Greece during this time. Upon his death, tyranny (the rule) of Athens was passed to Peisistratus's son, Hippias.

Hippias began his career much in step with that of his father's rule. He ruled with a modicum of respect and good-treatment of the people of Athens. However, when his brother was murdered, Hippias became paranoid and vitriolic against the people of Athens. He began to execute and banish people who either were, or who he thought were connected with his brother's murder. He took the new freedoms that the people had gained under Peisistratus and replaced it with oppression.

Cleisthenes began his involvement in the revolution of Athens around 510 BC with the intention of seizing power for himself. He had been brought up to further his self-interest, and followed this dictum to its end. Cleisthenes conspired, and succeeded in overthrowing Hippias, and the latter was banished from Athens.

The rule of Cleisthenes was, however, beset by its own conspirators and rivals. The chief rival of Cleisthenes was another Athenian aristocrat named Isagoras. Isagoras had long been involved with the Spartans, and was even rumored to have shared his wife with the king of Sparta. Isagoras appealed to the Spartans to aid him in deposing Cleisthenes, and the Spartans complied.

Sparta, which is most well known for its military prowess, was poised to make Athens a subject of its growing realm of influence. The warlike polis had already dominated its surrounding area for hundreds of square miles, and with Isagoras, a friend of Sparta, as the new ruler of Athens, its influence was set to grow even more.

Fearing the opposition of Cleisthenes and other aristocrats, Isagoras banished Cleisthenes from Athens along with some 700 other households, and it looked like he may never return to his home again. However, having had a taste of freedom under the rule of Peisistratus, the people of Athens revolted against Isagoras and his Spartan allies.

Isagoras and his forces sought refuge in The Acropolis for a period of two days. On the third day, however, he surrendered to the onslaught of the common Athenian people. The citizens of Athens had taken power from the despot (absolute ruler) and had claimed it for themselves. The year was 508 BC. The people recalled Cleisthenes, and the others who had been banished by Isagoras.

It was clear that Cleisthenes could not rule in the manner which had been so common in Athens and various other Greek city-states of the time. It had become apparent that the people must be able to have a say in how they were governed. Cleisthenes ordered a stone meeting area to be carved out of the rock some distance from The Acropolis where the people of the city, commoners and aristocrats alike, could meet and discuss the issues of Athens. It was here that Cleisthenes instituted a simple form of voting. The first instances of the voting process consisted of presenting a white pebble to indicate assent, and a black pebble to indicate disagreement with whatever proposal was before the people.

Issues were brought for a vote every nine days, and these issues encompassed every facet of governance in the polis. This was a pure democracy where the government was one of the people without a separate body to counter or inhibit the decision of the people. Issues such as the declaration of war, raising or lowering taxes, all the way down to the prices of produce and other goods were decided by these democratic votes.

Not only would the advent of democracy give the common people as much of a say in the nature and direction of their government, it would create a system which would change the way that people of the area, and indeed the world after it, would view people's rights, and responsibilities in their own governance. Forms of democracy are still present today, and in its purest forms, it gives people the ability to have an actual, not only a perceived say, in what the government does.

While larger governments that take on a semblance of democracy today often rely heavily on the ideas of a republic (a system where officials are either elected or appointed to represent their individual areas such as representatives in the United States, or members of The House of Commons in Britain,) for the day to day issues and votes, as it would be wildly inefficient to hold votes with the general population every time an issue was presented, the earliest Greek democracy was a direct democracy which did incorporate this widespread influence of the people in every facet of governmental affairs.

The rise of democracy in Athens paved the way for the golden age of Greece. Culture after the advent of democracy in Athens and, subsequently, the rest of Greece flourished in a way that it never had before this time period.

There is evidence of other proto-democratic governments prior to the advent of Athenian democracy, however, the system instituted by Cleisthenes and his fellows was certainly the first of its kind. Not everyone in Athens had the right to vote however. Voting was intended only for adult males, although it's suspected that a voter's family may have had a good deal of influence on his vote.

Another influence that reached voters in a dramatic way (no pun intended) was the satire of the comedic poets of the time. These poets, like artists today, found the ability to sway public opinion in a very real way, and they would often use this power to turn votes to favor their own opinions.

Democracy, although popular among a good share of the people, was considered to be fallacious by many including the great philosopher Plato. Plato believed that unless elected officials were philosophers of the finest thread, Greece would never be free of the evils of ambition and tyranny. Plato favored a kingdom ruled by men of philosophy to ensure continual progress and rescue from the necessary evils contained in men who failed to question.

Another interesting facet of Athenian democracy was that of ostracism. Ostracism, put simply, was the voted ejection of a person from the borders of the city-state. Although the practice had the potential to rid the area of individuals who would be counterproductive to the spread of Greek freedoms, it was often used as a political tool to oust individuals who were unliked by an individual or a group. This process was often unofficially sanctioned for such means, as in the case of Themistocles, the great general who had led the Athenians to many important victories against Persia.

Although Athenian democracy wasn't perfect, it undoubtedly led to the Golden Age of Greece. People were brought together more through this simple invention, the casting of a stone, than they had been in the previous history of the land. Not only culture, but trade, production, the economy, and many other facets of Greek life were enhanced by this revolutionary concept.

CHAPTER 4

Darius, Xerxes, and the Persian Threat

In 492 BC, though the Democracy of Athens was still very young, Athens began to gain a significant amount of power. Athens at the time was still a smaller polis, but it caught the attention of Darius, known as The Great King of The Persian Empire.

The Persian Empire was undoubtedly the greatest power of the day. It was located across the sea to the East of Athens, and stretched from Turkey all the way to India. The Empire was ruled by Darius, a tyrannical leader who demanded unyielding submission. Darius was so feared by his people, and had such a level of dominion over them that those who would beg his favor were required to cover their mouths when in his presence so the air that he breathed would not be contaminated by their presence.

As all dictatorial rulers do, Darius feared the growth in power of any civilization other than his own. When it became clear that Athens was becoming too powerful for Darius's liking, he sent a force to invade.

The first campaign of the Persians against the Greeks was carried out by Mardonius, the son-in-law of Darius. During this campaign, Mardonius's forces conquered and re-subjugated the city of Thrace. Macedon, an ally of the Persians, was also subjugated. This campaign, although having its victories would end after the Persian fleet was lost in a storm near the coast of Mount Athos. After being injured during a raid of his camp, Mardonius returned home.

Darius sent ambassadors to all of the poleis of Greece demanding submission to his rule in 491, and almost all of these city-states complied. In Sparta and Athens, however, not only were the ambassadors refused their submission, but were also killed.

Undoubtedly the most famous event of the war between Darius's Persia and the city-states of Greece was the battle of Marathon. The Persians landed in the polis of Marathon, a city which had no standing army. News of the Persian invasion travelled quickly. The Persian Empire was one of tyranny and slavery, while the Greek city-states were a culture which valued its freedom.

That being so, a herald (or day runner/courier) named Pheidippides was sent from Athens to request the aid of Sparta, the military superpower of the Greek poleis, in dispelling the Persian force from their shores. Pheidippides ran over 150 miles (246 kilometers) in the space of less than two days. This remarkable journey through the countryside of Greece is the origin of modern marathons.

Although Pheidippides performed an astonishing feat by making this desperate run, the Spartans refused the plea for help. Athens would have to defend itself against the Persians.

While Pheidippides was making his run, the Athenians were gathering their forces. Everyone who was able from peasants armed with spears, sticks, or whatever they could find to the hoplites who were citizen-soldiers, able to afford the finer armor. The hoplites were predominantly armed with spears, clad in armor of bronze, and generally had some military training.

Despite being outnumbered two-to-one by the Persian forces, the Greek soldiers won an unlikely victory against their invaders. They killed an estimated 6,000 Persian troops in one day, and scattered their forces.

The victory of the Greeks over the Persians was an incredible blow to Darius. After the loss to the Greeks in the failed first invasion, Darius began amassing yet another enormous army. This army was intended to invade Greece yet again, but it fell into discord when the Egyptians revolted. Darius died while trying to quell this uprising. With Darius's death in 486 BC, control of The Persian Empire was passed to his son Xerxes.

Xerxes was hateful toward the Greeks and the Egyptians, blaming them for the death of his father. The revolt in Egypt was quickly put down by Xerxes, and a new plan to invade Greece was initiated. He decided to bridge Hellespont (modern day Dardanelles) a thin sea strait about .75 miles (1.2 kilometers) at its thinnest point in order for his massive army to cross into Greece.

Many of the Greek poleis pledged to voluntarily join with Xerxes and the Persian Empire when the Persians arrived. This campaign was delayed however, with a new revolt breaking out in Egypt.

Xerxes began to assemble his army after about four years of preparation. Although the Greek historian Herodotus's estimation of the size of the Persian force was most likely exaggerated, (a figure of 200,000 is much more likely than the stated number of 2.5 million) the size of the Persian army was the largest force of its day.

Xerxes sent ambassadors to the Greek city-states demanding food, water, and land as evidence of their submission to his rule. These ambassadors, due to the previous experience with Sparta and Athens, decided to stay away from those two city-states, hoping to prevent them from being prepared for the coming invasion. This plan did not work, however, as other Greek poleis which were opposed to Xerxes rule over their city-states banded together to form an alliance against the Persian onslaught.

Although only about 10% of the roughly 700 different Greek city-states joined, this alliance would become a powerful foreshadowing of Greek unification. At this time, the Greek poleis were loosely affiliated with one another, if at all. Many of these city-states were even at war with one another. Not much is known about the inner-workings of this confederation, however it is known that among the alliance's powers was that of sending troops to a location after consulting the matter.

In 480 BC, a mere six years after his rise to power, Xerxes's army crossed over their pontoon bridges at Hellespont into Greece. The Greek alliance planned to send its troops to defend against Xerxes's advance at the Vale of Tempe, however this plan was abandoned with news of the tactical risks.

Themistocles, a great Athenian general, proposed a second plan. In order to reach the Southern part of Greece, Xerxes would have to funnel his forces through the narrow pass of Thermopylae (hot gateways.) Themistocles suggested that the larger Persian force could be stopped were the Greeks to send its hoplites to block the pass. In addition, the Greek ships would block the sea strait of Artemisium to ensure that the Persian forces couldn't sidestep the pass of Thermopylae by sea.

The plan had a hitch though, as the estimated arrival of the Persian forces to Thermopylae would coincide with not only the Olympic games, but also with the festival of Carneia. Carneia took place between August (the Greek month of Carneus) 7th and the 15th. This was a festival to honor Apollo Carneus, and was of particular importance to the Spartans. Due to the observance of this festival, and the perceived sacrilege implied by committing warfare during this period, the Spartan force consisted only of King Leonidas and his personal bodyguard of 300 men.

The usual hippeus (Spartan royal honor guard) consisted of young men, but as the destruction of his force was all but assured, the guard was replaced by men who had already fathered children. Along with the Spartan force of 301 men (Counting Leonidas,) there was a supporting army of the allies who joined the defense of Thermopylae. Additional forces were gathered along their way.

Upon their arrival at Thermopylae, the allied army rebuilt the Phocian wall at the tightest place in the pass. Xerxes waited for three days for the men to leave the pass. It wasn't until he was finally convinced that this small force intended to hold the hot gateways that Xerxes sent his men to attack.

Despite overwhelming numbers, the allies had a few key elements on their side. Due to the narrowness of the pass, the larger force of the Persian army was forced to meet the phalanx (a close, usually rectangular formation of soldiers) of the Greeks straight on, causing their men to fall quickly at the hands of the superior tactic of the allied army. Also, the Spartans, despite their smaller numbers, were exceptionally well-trained, as they were brought up from childhood to be soldiers. They also had, surprisingly enough, a great amount of morale due to the knowledge that they were choosing to fight (and die) by their own choice, and the invading force was one of slaves and conscripted men.

The allied forces held out against the massive Persian armies for a period of two days until a local man named Ephialtes betrayed them by disclosing a path behind the Greek forces to Xerxes. Leonidas caught wind of the betrayal, and released the larger part of the combined army, keeping only his men and a handful of other volunteers, leaving a grand total of about 2,000 men to cover the retreat of the rest of the forces. According to Herodotus, these men stood defiant against the prospect of certain destruction. Xerxes, not wanting to lose any more of his men, called upon his archers to deliver the final blow against the allied forces at Thermopylae.

Although this battle was lost, one crucial thing came of it. The Greeks began to see that unification could and would be to the benefit of the poleis, so long as these cities were allowed to keep their freedom.

While the battle of Thermopylae was taking place, another impressive battle was being carried out on the seas. Xerxes's navy was engaged in a naval battle against 271 allied Greek triremes. The Greeks were covering the flank of the army at Thermopylae. The allied navy held up against the Persian onslaught for the space of about three days until, hearing of the outcome of the battle at Thermopylae, the damaged allied vessels retreated as they were no longer needed.

After Thermopylae, Xerxes went on to conquer all of Boeotia, and subsequently most of Greece. Themistocles hatched a desperate plan. Before the first battle, he had consulted with the oracle at Delphi. The message from the Delphic oracle was as follows:

"Now your statues are standing and pouring sweat. They shiver with dread. The black blood drips from the highest rooftops. They have seen the necessity of evil. Get out, get out of my sanctum and drown your spirits in woe." (Fontenrose, 1981)

The message was a great blow to the Greeks, however, when consulted again, the oracle gave them a way out:

"A wall of wood alone shall be uncaptured, a boon to you and your children." (Fontenrose, 1981)

The city-state of Athens had no wooden walls at this time, but Themistocles took the second divination as the Greeks' way to victory. He believed that the wall of wood described a force of Greek Triremes, the most advanced ships in the armada. He commissioned hundreds of these ships to be made, and the beginning stages of his plan began to come together.

When Xerxes and his forces advanced toward Athens, Themistocles convinced them to do something drastic. The Athenians evacuated their homes and ultimately their city. Athens fell to the Persians, and their homes, temples, and most of the city was destroyed. Xerxes, frustrated at having received more resistance than he had hoped for, decided that his best bet in ending the conflict quickly was to destroy the Greek armada.

Led by Themistocles, the force of Greek triremes was stationed off the coast of Salamis, and Themistocles put his plan into action. He sent Xerxes a note disguised as a treasonous missive which told Xerxes of the armada's location. What he didn't convey was that the Greeks had hoped for Xerxes's armada to join battle with the Greek triremes in this place because, much like at Thermopylae, the superior Persian numbers would be forced to attack the Greeks in a narrow strait, thereby levelling the playing field.

The plan worked. According to Herodotus, Xerxes sat upon his throne on a beach, watching the naval battle commence. His fleet was torn apart by that of the Greeks, and the battle was lost. It's said that about 200 Persian ships were sunk or captured by the Greek navy, and the battle was a red-letter victory for the forces of Greece.

Xerxes, infuriated at the loss of his naval superiority fled back to his empire, leaving Mardonius, his brother-in-law to complete the subjugation and conquest of Greece. Although the war was not yet over, the Greeks would prevail against the Persian forces, and return to their homes after the battle of Salamis-in-Cyprus.

In 478 BC, The Delian League was formed to ally various poleis against the threat of Persia after the second invasion. Somewhere between 150 and 172 individual city-states came together to form the Delian league. This group got its modern name from their meeting place on the island of Delos. Athens grew rich and powerful through its influence in the league and, much to the chagrin of smaller, less powerful states, grew to a great deal of overall superiority. It wasn't long after the inception of the Delian League Athens took control of the league's navy, and the Athenian proclivity toward heavy-handed tactics for its own interest led to the Peloponnesian War. The league was disbanded at the conclusion of this war.

These years of conflict with the Persians had certainly taken their toll on Greece and its people, however, with victory came a new kind of unification among the Greek poleis, and gave rise to the golden age of Greece.

CHAPTER 5

Pericles and the Golden Age

Also called the classical age, the golden age of Greece lasted between about 480-300 BC. Although the Athenians and the Spartans came together to fight the Persians, they would remain rivals throughout most of their existence in the ancient times.

Much of the history that we have of Greece was recorded by a man named Herodotus (484-409 BC.) He was a historian, in fact, he's often known as the father of history (although Voltaire would later refer to him as the father of lies.) Herodotus was the first known historian to not only retell, or collect history, but to take certain measures to test the authenticity of the stories of the day and of the past.

The golden age of Greece was a veritable explosion of philosophy, art, and architecture. This period was home not only to Herodotus, but to philosophers such as Socrates, Plato, and Aristotle, men whose insights would not only change the thoughts of the day, but live on to affect us in modern times. We will get to them in the next chapter.

Discussion of the golden age of Greece cannot be in any way thorough without taking a look at Pericles. Pericles (495-429 BC) began taking part in politics in Athens around 472 BC. As son to a well-known politician, a man by the name of Xanthippus, Pericles was encouraged at a young age to become involved with politics and government.

Athens was still reeling from the impact of the wars with Persia, and it was a long and difficult process toward rebuilding and restoring order. Pericles saw the wealth that was accruing to Athens through the Delian League, and contrasted this with the fact that Athens had not been fully rebuilt. Rather than add to the force of the navy by manpower, or construction of triremes, many of the city-states in the Delian League elected instead to donate money and other provisions. With this wealth, the city of Athens was poised, not only for rebuilding, but for a large-scale glorification of their city.

Although, after continued campaigns by the Delian League against Persia had rendered the former foe inconsequential as a threat to the Greeks at the time, Pericles insisted that the other members of the dissolving council continue to donate as they had when military campaigns were at their height. Pericles eventually raided the stockpile of wealth at Delos and brought it to his home polis of Athens.

With this influx of wealth, Pericles had the city and its temples restored. Along with this, he commissioned the building of the Parthenon, a site which, although in ruins today, still holds a great deal of interest to Athens and indeed the world. The Parthenon housed an enormous statue of Athena, and was certainly an incomparable testament to the artistry and craftsmanship of the day. No expense was spared, and it is interesting to note that the Parthenon doesn't actually contain any right angles. It was built in such a way as to compensate for the illusion which is created by intersecting lines that makes them appear to bow.

It is often said, as Thucydides once remarked, that Athens during this time was only a democracy in its appearance, while in actuality, it was ruled by Pericles, sometimes known as The First Citizen of Athens.

With the outbreak of the Peloponnesian War, a conflict between Athens and its allies against Sparta and its allies which lasted approximately 30 years, not only would the supremacy of Athens come under fire, but the control of Athens by the Athenians was also culled.

The Peloponnesian war began when Athens made it apparent that Persia was not to fear, Athens was. The parties of the Delian League were taken advantage of by the Athenians and Sparta wasn't willing to trade one dictator abroad for one closer to home. The most complete account of the Peloponnesian war was made by General Thucydides, an aforementioned ally of Pericles.

Athens basically controlled the Delian League however Sparta, never to be outdone, had its own league called The Peloponnesian League. The Peloponnesian League was vast and powerful. When the helots, Sparta's slave class, revolted in 465 BC, Athens sent a force to support the Spartans, however their assistance was refused as Sparta believed the force was intended, not to aid Sparta, but to take advantage of the conflict.

In 449, two members of the Peloponnesian League came into conflict. Athens and Megara formed an alliance and decided to enter into the conflict. This resulted in Spartan forces pitting themselves against Athens, and is often referred to as the First Peloponnesian War. The outcome of this conflict ended in 445 BC with an agreement of peace between the two empires known as the 30 Years Peace. The terms set down basically came down to the Athenian Empire and the Spartan Empires agreeing to not get involved with matters of their respective groups.

The Athenians, however, did not long hold to this agreement and set about involving themselves in acts such as taking over settlements, imposing sanctions, and striking out against the Peloponnesian League at large. Under Pericles, a wall was built between Athens and its port of Piraeus so that Athens, even if besieged by Sparta, would be able to import whatever goods it required from its growing empire, and it would never have to meet the fierce Spartan army on its own terms. Due to Athenian naval superiority, it was able to move much more quickly than the Spartan army, and even bypass it entirely. For this purpose, much of the Spartan force was required to stay in and around Sparta for fear of an Athenian attack. Athens, Pericles theorized, would remain safe so long as it didn't attempt to expand its empire.

Unfortunately for Athens, the construction of this wall encased the citizens of the polis in close quarters, and in a relatively short amount of time, these close quarters along with a lack of general sanitation led to an outbreak of plague which killed an estimated 30,000 Athenian citizens. Pericles himself succumbed to this plague, and died within six months of contracting it.

With the death of Pericles, rule of the city went to various demagogues until Alcibiades took control of the polis. He went against the non-expansion which Pericles had insisted upon and sought to grow the Athenian Empire. Alcibiades led a campaign to take Sicily which was, at that time, under attack from Syracuse. Upon his return, however, Alcibiades went, not back to the Athenians, but to Sparta. His allegiance would switch many times between alliance to Athens and allegiance to Sparta, no doubt weakening the cause of Athens.

Alcibiades was eventually killed, not just for his ambivalent alliances to Greek States, but also at times with Persia. The Athenians were caught in a state of discord as many leaders would follow Alcibiades in their lust for control over the Athenian Empire. Multiple further campaigns were sent to Sicily, and all of them failed, eventually decimating the naval supremacy of Athens. This wouldn't be the last word on the Athenian navy, however, as they built new ships and formed new armies.

Things finally turned after the battle of Arginusae. Although the Athenian fleet had won a great battle, the brilliant naval commanders were executed due to their retreat from a storm in order to save their ships. Without the skilled leadership of these commanders, the Athenian Navy was eventually decimated by a Spartan fleet that sailed in Persian ships. The polis of Athens would eventually be starved into submission.

This Spartan victory led to the end of the war in 404 BC and the eventual subjugation of Athens by Sparta. A group known as the 30 tyrants who led Athens now, not in a democracy as it had been, but an oligarchy (rule by a small group of people.) This oligarchy would not stand however, as Athens was eventually able to retake their city and their democracy about a year after the institution of the 30 tyrants.

This war was costly to both sides, and eventually led to the fall of both poleis to outside forces.

In the north, a city called Macedon was not far from coming to a level of power as yet unknown in Greece, or indeed the world. Macedon had long battled against barbarian invaders, and had fallen into bad a rapport with the more influential city-states of the time. The Macedonians were often considered to be hardly civilized themselves, but it would be the successive reign of one man and his son that would change the political and cultural landscape of the world.

Philip II (382-336 BC) came to power in 359 BC. Philip had a vision for Macedon and for Greece itself. He wasted no time in getting his plans off the ground. The common practice of warfare in Greece at the time was based on the phalanx formation, and Philip's armies were no different in that fundamental aspect. However, it was the development of weaponry, diplomatic relations, and a change to a professional, well trained army that would make these plans possible.

Macedon had lost key battles before Philip II's accession to the throne. Philip was quick to forge alliances with neighboring cities and set about rebuilding the army. He not only rebuilt the army in numbers, but oversaw the development of a few different types of weapons that would make the Macedonian military the envy of the world. One of these weapons was called the sarissa.

The sarissa was a pike, or long spear, up to about 20 feet in length. Used in a phalanx and in conjunction with cavalry units, the sarissa could keep enemy forces at bay and at a distance while they were being flanked. Enemies had nothing to match the length of the sarissa, and were more often than not at the mercy of the Macedonian forces at the tips of these pikes.

Another important innovation was that of the gastraphetes (belly-shooters.) Unlike the traditional bow and arrow that only had as much force as the archer had strength in his arms, gastraphetes were crossbows which harnessed the power of a man's whole body. These weapons were a far sight more powerful and more effective against enemy units, especially in siege operations, than bows and arrows.

Along with sarissas and gastraphetes, two types of torsion ballistae were developed: oxybeles (bolt-shooters) and lithobolos (stone-shooters.) The oxybeles could fling a large bolt to lengths of up to a quarter mile, and easily penetrate enemy armor. The lithobolos could hurl stones up to 180 pounds in weight a great distance, effectively making the Macedonian forces unmatched in distance warfare.

One of Philip's sons, a young man who would grow to join his father on his military campaigns, and eventually become king was named Alexander. Alexander (more commonly referred to as Alexander the Great) came under the tutelage of Aristotle, a well-known and important philosopher at the age of 13.

When his father was battling against Byzantium, Alexander was left in charge. A group called the Maedi staged a revolt against Macedonia, and Alexander was put to an early test. He quickly drove the Maedi from their land and settled his own countrymen in their place and founded Alexandropolis, the first, but far from the last city that Alexander would name for himself.

By 346 BC, Philip's power had grown to a level which, in practice, set him as the leader of Greece. The Greek city-states resented the reach of Philip's power, and began to build their resistance to him. In 338 BC, allied Greek poleis, including Athens and Thebes, fought against Philip and Alexander in the battle of Chaeronea.

Alexander was only 18 at the time of the battle, and when he and his father prevailed against the forces of Athens and Thebes, Philip was in a position to destroy or rule these city-states in whatever way he so desired. In a gesture that was completely unexpected by these conquered city-states, Philip allowed the men to return to their homes and carry on within their cities as they had done before the conflict. Philip loved the culture of Greece, and wished for the territories he had conquered to retain their individuality.

Philip would die in 336 BC, just before mounting his ultimate plan of invading the vast and powerful empire of Persia, at the hands of one of his own bodyguards. During his 20 years ruling Macedon, Philip had made his once looked-down-upon city the seat of the Greek Empire. Alexander, now 20, would take the throne of Macedon.

Being only half-Macedonian himself and having a slew of relatives (Philip had seven wives, only one of which was Macedonian,) Alexander had rivals for the succession to his father's throne. His first order of duty was to remove the contentious parties, many of them by death.

Once secured as king, Alexander followed in his father's footsteps and set out to conquer Greek's longtime enemy of Persia. Before he set off to the east, he put down a number of rebellions, including that of Thebes and Athens.

With the seat of his power secure, Alexander set off for Persia. The Persian Empire stretched from the Middle East to parts of Asia and included portions of

Northern Africa, most notably Egypt. Alexander's task was an enormous one, but he showed his intentions famously by striking a spear into the ground in Asia and proclaimed that he accepted the land as a gift from the gods.

Alexander would win multitudinous victories, cutting his way through the Persian Empire, assaulting Persian cities and harbors, rendering Persian naval forces ineffectual. One of the most impressive victories on his way through the Persian Empire was at the battle of Tyre.

Tyre was a largely fortified city in the Mediterranean Sea that was proving to be difficult to take due to its distance from the shore. The port of Tyre was the last remaining harbor in the region still in his enemy's hands, and so Alexander wasn't about to abandon his campaign against the city.

He made a couple of offers to the Tyrians to avoid full-on conflict. One was that he would leave the people their lives if he was allowed to make a sacrifice at the temple of Melqart, as he equated Melqart with Heracles. He then sent representatives to discuss an agreement of peace, but they were killed and thrown from the city walls into the sea.

Alexander ordered that a siege be staged against the city, and he built a causeway, roughly 2/3 of a mile long (1 kilometer) to the Tyrian shore. With the use of siege towers, he eventually took the city and, frustrated by the stubbornness of the Tyrians, he set fire to the city.

Alexander continued his campaigns and before he was done, he was hailed as King of Macedonia (336-323 BC), Pharaoh of Egypt (332-323 BC), King of Asia (331-323 BC), and King of Persia (330-323 BC.)

Alexander died of an unknown illness in 323 BC. Accounts differ on some of the specifics, such as whether or not he had a fever. There were claims that he was poisoned, but these were largely discounted as he lived for nearly two weeks after taking ill. His military campaigns and his reign over much of the known world would become the stuff of legend.

The Classical Age of Greece effectively came to an end with Alexander's death.

Although this time period was often rife with conflict, it also produced many of the most fantastical wonders of the Greek world. Culture flourished, and many of the Athenian arts, architecture, and philosophies are still something to marvel at to this day.

CHAPTER 6

Philosophy and Discord

Socrates was often described as a plainly ugly man who travelled around wearing a single robe. He was born an Athenian in 469 BC, and would live until his sentence of death by hemlock was carried out in 399 BC. Despite his genius, Socrates was illiterate and therefore his words were collected by Plato and Xenophon, two of his students. Along with his incredible mind, Socrates was also known for his strength, and he fought in the Peloponnesian War.

Although Socrates was an incredibly astute man, when he was proclaimed by the Oracle of Delphi to be the wisest man in all of Athens, he was taken aback, and postulated that either all men must be equally ignorant, or that he was wise by his awareness of his ignorance. His penchant for getting lost in thought was the stuff of legend, and he is claimed to have gotten so wrapped up in his thoughts one day that he stood in one spot, unmoving for the entire length of that day.

His philosophy was one of free-thinking, and questioning the ideas presented through logical processes, each for himself or herself. The Socratic method was a practice of discussion and critical thinking that was intended to question even one's own thoughts and opinions and checking them for their plausibility. Elenchus (proving an idea false by showing its opposite to be true) was the predominant form of Socratic criticism.

In 399 BC, the tyrants of Athens were overthrown. Although Socrates had often shown himself to be a friend to the people of Athens, only suggesting that they look within and without themselves to challenge their beliefs, he was accused of poisoning the minds of the children. He was held for trial, and acted in his own defense. The "courts" of the time were much different than those with which we are familiar today. He was given a brief period in which to defend himself, and used this time to logically prove that he wasn't subject to trial and, in fact, should be honored with free food for the remainder of his life, and held as a benefactor of the people. The judges weren't pleased with his defense and found him guilty, sentencing him to death by hemlock. It was said by his student Xenophon that Socrates's defiance was intentional with the purpose to offend the judges and secure a guilty verdict. According to Xenophon, Socrates believed that he was better off dead.

Socrates was jailed for about a month, but was allowed visitors. The hemlock poison which Socrates was to drink caused an extremely painful death, however when his friends came to him before he drank the poison, he spent his time peacefully discussing the immortality of the soul. Socrates actually had a chance to escape the city, and thus, his sentence, as his friends successfully bribed a guard, but Socrates refused to leave. He reasoned that, even were his verdict to be unfair, it was more important to obey these laws even if it meant his death. Otherwise, the state would have come to harm by this flight from captivity. He willingly drank the hemlock potion dry.

It is postulated by some that Socrates was not in fact a real man, but a creation of Plato. The argument is that Plato formulated the great philosopher in order to give added weight to his own theories. Although there is still debate today about the actual existence of the man named Socrates, the fact remains that his philosophies, whether formulated by himself as a real man, or by Plato as a means to further his own career, have had an enormous impact not only in the time of his life, but throughout the ages, continuing to this day.

Plato (born somewhere between 428 and 423 BC, and died around 347 BC) was a great philosopher and student of Socrates, is quite possibly the most influential philosopher of all time. Plato's prolific written work was not purveyed in the manner to which we are commonly accustomed, but set down as a series of events which usually contained a debate between philosophers.

Plato's ideal government was one where enlightened philosophers would be elevated to the level of kings, as it was only the philosophers who could justly rule. Believing, as Socrates was purported to have said (paraphrased here), that a life without questioning one's beliefs is not a life worth living; it's no leap to understand why Plato favored this form of government, although it would never take form.

One of his predominant philosophies was that of The Theory of Forms. Although this philosophy is now widely discredited, it was often central to Platonic thought. The gist of this philosophy is that what we can perceive is not, in fact, the solid nature of things, but rather (as he would state in the cave analogy) that they are mere shadows *of* the purified forms which are invisible to us.

Plato also believed that knowledge isn't acquired, rather, it is *remembered*. Plato postulated that originally, we had the full and complete knowledge of every aspect of existence, however, we would lose these things and any knowledge that we might gain throughout our lives was a mere remembrance of previously known things.

Although these are a few examples of Platonic thought, this is by no means intended to be a comprehensive list of Plato's philosophy.

A student of Plato, a philosopher by the name of Aristotle (384-322 BC), was regarded to be one of the well-versed philosophers, not only of the ancient world, but of all time. Although, as with many of the ancient philosophers, a large part of his philosophical theories have been discarded, he was and is a very influential man in the field of philosophy. Although a student of Plato, Aristotle rejected the Theory of Forms.

One of Aristotle's philosophies was that of incidental and essential features. For instance, a rock can be black, brown, red, or green and it is still a rock. This would be an example of an incidental feature. However, a rock's composition would be a necessary feature, as a rock made out of feathers would not, in actuality, be a rock.

Aristotle developed a method called formal logic which is still widely used today. The use of formal logic can be illustrated by use of syllogism. This method postulates that new knowledge can be deduced by the combination of previously verified truths. An example would be: All men are six feet tall. John is a man. If John is a man, then he is six feet tall. In this example is also illustrated a further part of formal logic which is that if one of the two propositions is found to be untrue, then the conclusion cannot be said to be necessarily true itself. In this case, it's not true that all men are six feet tall, therefore it can only be deduced from this information that some men may be six-feet tall, but men (including John) aren't necessarily of this height.

Aristotle also believed that any statement could only be true or false. The problem with this philosophy, however, arises when postulating future-oriented statements. If one person says that they were going to walk to the store and randomly meet a tall woman named Daphne and another person said that he would not meet such a woman, but a short man named Bruce then which one of them was telling the truth? Before the event, this is unknowable. Another problem arises if, when arriving at the store, the first person actually does meet a short man named Bruce, this person can't argue that the other was wrong in their statement, even though the result happened out of mere happenstance.

These are but a few examples of a few of the theories of a few of the philosophers of the day. Philosophy during this time was highly revered, and these men (and many others) made an indelible mark on the world with their ideas.

CHAPTER 7

Enter the Roman Empire

Greek sovereignty was not to last forever. Many invaders entered and conquered various states of Greece; however the Roman conquest of Greece would prove the largest empirical change to the region for many years to come.

The Punic wars lasted from 264 to 146 BC and were predominantly a conflict between Rome in modern day Italy and Carthage in northern Africa. Although, during the Third Punic War, the conflict wasn't contained in the land-mass of Greece, the Romans had become increasingly irritated by the agitation of the Greek states.

The growing Roman power had fought many battles within the land of Greece; however, it was the Roman conquest of the city of Corinth that brought things to a head. The Romans fought against the Corinthians and their allies of the second Achaean League, a confederation of Greek city-states in the north-central area of Peloponnese.

The Romans, well known as fierce expansionists, finally took the City of Corinth in 146 BC, and although this was not the immediate end of the Greek empire, it was the first major blow toward this end. Although the Achaean League revolted against its Roman invaders, the onslaught of the Romans was only beginning.

Not only were cities taken, but the Greek religion was absorbed and equated with that of the Romans. Deities such as Zeus, Aphrodite, and Ares were equated with Jupiter, Venus, and Mars respectively. This cultural shift played a big part in the Romanization of the Greek empire.

The Greek Peninsula at large would come under the control of Rome or its prefecture in 146 BC with the Aegean Islands following suit in 133 BC. Greece had long been influential in Roman life and culture. Under the rule of Rome, Greek culture was actually much the same as it had been. This continuity of Greek culture lasted until the arrival of Christianity, even though Greek independence was ended.

Greece and Rome were long intertwined, not necessarily as allied forces, but as a sharing of cultures. This is by no means to suggest that these cultures didn't clash with each other, although there was often a level of give-and-take on this cultural level.

CONCLUSION

We have arrived at the conclusion of this section. I want to thank you for joining me on this incredible journey through one of the greatest civilizations that our world has ever seen.

History, even ancient history such as this, is important, not only because it tells us where we came from and what affected the world of the past, but it has shaped all of us, Greek or no in our societies and our cultures.

From the philosophers such as Socrates, Plato, and Aristotle to the military leaders such as Thucydides, Leonidas, and Philip II, the times and places associated with Ancient Greece have left their indelible imprint on our world, and indeed, on all of us who live in it.

With history, we find myth and fact, truth and legend about the people who lived during these far away times. We also find in our own civilizations today marks of those seemingly distant times. By looking at the past, we can better understand our present, and plan for a better future with the lessons long ago learned, passed down through countless generations of men and women whose own lives form a lineage, a direct connection with those times.

It has been an absolute pleasure to delve into this elegant, often troubled time in the history of the world and share with you a collection of some of the events that took place to shape an incredible empire.

From its humble beginnings to the unprecedented reign of Alexander the Great, Greece has been a fascination of millions of people throughout the ages. I hope that you have enjoyed this journey as much as I have, and I hope that you'll press on with the other histories in this series to discover even more about the civilizations that have set the stage for our modern life.

When we look back into the past, we see ourselves in the cacophony of the times which have preceded our own. Peace and war, enlightenment and ignorance, and the individual journeys of the heroic and the common alike no doubt will continue to shape our world as we move forward, day by day, in our own quests for greatness.

PART 2
ANCIENT EGYPT

Ancient Secrets of the Egyptians

INTRODUCTION

Ancient Egypt is one of the most fascinating civilizations that the world has ever seen. From looming
pyramids to intricate monoliths; from kings and
pharaohs to the waters of the Nile, Egypt's history is
one in which we can see the potential of humanity.

Even today, while there are some theories, we are not
certain how the ancient Egyptians built many of their
monuments, including the pyramids. The civilization
of Egypt was home to some of the most profound
thought of the time, some of the most incredible in-
ventions and some of the most famous rulers
throughout history.

So what is it about Ancient Egypt that has fascinated
us for millennia and continues to pique our interest
today?

There seems to be a unique spirit to the ancient Egyptians. The Egyptian way of life seems to be almost
anachronistic in a lot of ways. They had primitive
batteries (we still don't know why,) they were fans of
board games, women enjoyed more freedom in ancient Egypt than they did in other civilizations, in

many cases for thousands of years to come, they had house pets, used a form of chewing gum made from myrrh and wax and some Egyptian doctors actually specialized in different areas of medicine.

Providing exact dates to events in ancient Egypt can be quite difficult, and in some cases impossible, as the ancient Egyptians did not use a standardized system of chronology as we do today. The ancient Egyptians would instead use the length of their pharaohs' reigns as a way of telling the year. While this may have been useful enough at the time, it's difficult for researchers nowadays to pinpoint at exactly which time the fourth year of Khufu was. In most cases we don't know exactly when these pharaohs reigned, or even how close we are to a complete list of pharaohs. Therefore, dates in this book will focus more on a dynastic timeline with modern calendar years being added in where possible.

The history, culture and symbolism of ancient Egypt is still popular today, over two thousand years later. There are many things to be fascinated about in regard to ancient Egypt. But what made them who they were? What drove them to settle where they settled, live how they lived and create such an enigmatic and captivating civilization? How were the Egyptians able to sustain their civilization for nearly three thousand years?

These and many other questions will be covered in these pages. I invite you to sit back, relax and enjoy learning about what is quite possibly the most important and interesting ancient civilizations the world has ever seen.

CHAPTER **8**

Agriculture and Moving Toward Dynasty

The history of ancient Egyptian civilization (or Kemet – The Black Land as it was known during the Old Kingdom) begins and ends with the Nile River, referred to in ancient Egypt as Iteru, or Great River. It is the largest river in the world in regard to length. (The Amazon drains more water, but the Nile is longer.) The Nile is not only notable for its length, but its regularity, its navigability and its smooth currents. This is such an important thing to Egypt (ancient and present) because of its use in agriculture.

Egypt for the most part is a desert, but with the fertile water of the Nile which floods every year, people were able to set up settlements and a whole civilization around its shores. The silt and mineral deposits left by the flooding of the Nile literally made the ground so fertile that ancient Egyptians would cast their seeds over the soft earth and let their livestock walk over it, thereby "planting" their crops.

The civilizations of Egypt were primarily right along the banks of the river. The navigability of the river allowed the inhabitants to send resources along its currents for trade, and the fertile land made crop-growing easy enough that people had more time to focus on different aspects of their lives.

The Nile wasn't without its perils however. Along with alligators and crocodiles, the yearly flooding was often unpredictable in size. Some years this led to increased flooding which would deluge towns and cities along the Nile River Valley. At others, the flood would not be high enough; crops would suffer and people would starve.

Prior to wide-spread settling along the Nile River Valley, the peoples of Egypt were largely nomadic. They would hunt large prey in the fertile lands of the Sahara (this is before it became the world's biggest desert.) This all changed with the climate shift of approximately 5,000 B.C. The land dried up and larger animals were unable to continue to live in the area. The Nile quickly became the only source of water in the area.

Before Egypt was united, it consisted of Upper Egypt and Lower Egypt. Upper Egypt is called as such due to its location nearer the source of the Nile River. The rulers of Upper Egypt wore a long, white crown. This crown was known as the Hedjet. It symbolized power and divine right to the subjects of Upper Egypt.

Lower Egypt began at the Mediterranean Sea in the north and ran upstream on the Nile to the south, meeting its end at the boundary of Upper Egypt with a cataract, or river rapid near Aswan. The kings of Lower Egypt wore a red crown called the Deshret. It too represented a divine right, and one or both crowns were often depicted on the god Horus, who was believed to be the ruler from whom the kings and pharaohs inherited the throne.

Why so much focus on the crowns of Upper and Lower Egypt? It was the unification of these crowns that would signify a unified Egypt. This begins with a man named Narmer. Narmer was king of Upper-Egypt. Historians are unsure if other rulers of the time were actually this man, or if Narmer was a representative of multiple kingships during the unification of Upper and Lower Egypt.

Most of what we know about Narmer can be traced back to the Narmer Palette. The Narmer Palette depicts Narmer with both crowns of Egypt and hitting an enemy with a flail or mace. It is the earliest depiction of a king wearing both crowns and thus suggests that the battle depicted in the palette was the final battle that granted him the kingship over both Upper and Lower Egypt.

As the story goes, however, Narmer (possibly Menes, Aha or Scorpion) unified the previously rival lands of

Upper and Lower Egypt in 3150 B.C. He did this through administrative and militaristic means. He was the first king to wear the double-crown, the crowns of Upper and Lower Egypt, the Hedjet and the Deshret. This symbolized the union of Egypt into one nation, ruled by a single man and unified through culture and political means.

Along with unifying Egypt, he also founded the city of Memphis – "Balance of Two Lands" (also called Inbu-Hedj meaning "white walls") which would serve as Egypt's capitol for many dynasties. A dynasty is a string of rulers, generally of the same bloodline. The city was surrounded on all sides by large walls. This protected the city from the flooding of the Nile while allowing it to be in the prime location for farming, trade and travel.

Narmer is said to have ruled for a period of about sixty years. During this time, Egypt became ever more united, religion and spirituality were promulgated and the land flourished. The death of Narmer is disputed today, but original records say that he was killed by a hippopotamus.

Along with the unification of Upper Egypt to the south and Lower Egypt to the north, the civilizations on the east and west sides of the river Nile would come to be unified. This was important to the Egyptians for religious reasons, due to their belief that in the East, where the sun rises, was symbolized new life, growth and prosperity, whereas the west, the direction of the setting sun, symbolized death and the afterlife. This can be noted throughout the civilization of the time as many burial grounds were located on the western banks of the Nile and the east contained most settlements and temples.

The rule of Narmer is commonly referred to as the dynasty 0.

Dynasties 1 and 2 comprise the time period most commonly known as the early dynastic period or the archaic period. It is during this time period that the earliest examples Egyptian writing can be found. This period is marked by the transition from a pre-dynastic Egypt to a civilization more familiar to us as Ancient Egypt. The archaic period lasted from around 3100-2686 BC.

CHAPTER 9

The Old Kingdom

Just like societies today, the social structure of the old kingdom was mostly made up of skilled and unskilled laborers, craftsmen, farmers, etc. This group made up the largest population by far, but these people enjoyed fewer rights and privileges than all of the other classes. Above them were the richer nobles and local leaders who enjoyed a level of affluence which escaped all but the luckiest of the working class members. Directly above the nobles in power were the priests, and above them sat the pharaoh.

It wasn't until the third dynasty that The Old Kingdom began. The old kingdom existed between 2686 and 2333 BC, and was a crucial period for the Egyptians. The old kingdom lasted between the third and sixth dynasties. It's during the old kingdom that we find some of the most iconic structures that the world has ever known: the pyramids.

It was in the third dynasty that King Djoser commissioned the first pyramid to be built. It was to be a burial tomb, and was created out of stone. This step-pyramid is located at Saqqara, and can still be seen today.

Although it wasn't until the fifth dynasty that texts would be set down to later be discovered by archaeologists regarding the funerary beliefs of the Ancient Egyptians, it's likely that these traditions went back a ways further, possibly to pre-dynastic Egypt.

Ancient Egyptians believed that a body must be preserved in order to reach the afterlife intact, and that even having an afterlife was decided by the gods, most notably, the pharaoh.

Viewed as not only a king, but the intermediary between the gods and man, the pharaoh wielded a great deal of power and demanded great respect, not only from the common people, but nobles as well. In order to reach the afterlife, it was considered necessary that an individual must have a purpose there. The pharaoh was a shoo-in, due to the fact of his leadership and pre-selection as a god among men. Along with the pharaoh, human sacrifices were common, usually so the pharaoh would have servants in the afterlife. Pretty bleak, huh? Along with this, it was necessary for a person to prove his or her worth in life so that they could be considered worthy of taking part in the afterlife.

One of the most predominant concepts of ancient belief was Ma'at: living a truthful, balanced, lawful, moral and just life. Ma'at was also a goddess in Ancient Egypt whose feather would be the counterweight placed against the weight of a person's heart. Those who lived just lives (those whose hearts weighed equal or less than that of Ma'at's feather) would enjoy an afterlife in paradise, or Aaru. Those whose hearts outweighed the feather would be doomed to live in the underworld (Duat) for eternity and the heart would be eaten by Ammit, the soul-eater. That's why it's a good idea to live a light-hearted life. (The author would like to apologize here; however, it should be noted that no history book is complete without at least one bad pun. Let's all hope that's the only one.)

As the in-depth mythological beliefs of the ancient Egyptians are investigated at length in another volume of this series, it is outside of the scope of this present work to delve too deeply into Egyptian mythology where it doesn't specifically concern the history of the Ancient Egyptians.

In earlier periods in Egypt, the dead were simply buried in the arid ground. This would preserve them due to a lack of moisture. Over time, those with a greater amount of affluence would be buried in small tombs called mastabas.

It was in these mastabas that the pharaohs before Djoser were buried. The issue with mastabas, however, was that the bodies would rot in a way that they hadn't in the arid ground, due to the cooler temperatures which caused a greater amount of moisture to collect inside them. This sent the Egyptians on the path toward a different kind of body-preservation, and one that comes quick to mind at the mere mention of ancient Egypt.

Mummification is the process of preserving the bodies through removal of the organs (although this was a later addition to the process,) use of embalming fluid and wrapping of the body in long strips of cloth. When embalmers did start to remove the organs (sometime around the fourth dynasty,) all of the organs (with the notable exception of the heart for reasons seen above) were removed in order to preserve it for the afterlife.

Not only were bodies that were considered worthy of a shot at the afterlife preserved, possessions of the dead were also buried with them. Depending on a person's wealth, these possessions would include coins, jewels, pots and other luxuries but also sometimes included servants and pets. It was believed that what a person was buried or entombed with would go with them into the afterlife.

For kings, pharaohs and richer nobles, mummification was a privilege, however, most commoners likely continued to be buried in the sand.

It was during the time of Djoser, however, that the first pyramid was built. Djoser's architect Imhotep (also a physician, engineer, chancellor to Djoser, a carpenter, sculptor and high-priest... imagine that paycheck) is credited with designing the first pyramid in Egypt, the above-mentioned Pyramid of Djoser at Saqqara. This would be the first, but far from the last or greatest pyramid constructed throughout Egypt.

It was during the fourth dynasty that some of the most recognizable pyramids were built. The first of the fourth dynasty's pharaohs, Sneferu is thought to have ordered the construction of up to three pyramids. It was his son Khufu, however, that would be responsible for ordering and overseeing construction of the great pyramid of Giza.

Although it is commonly thought that the pyramids were built by an enormous population of slaves, evidence suggests that this work was actually bought and paid for. Not much is known about the specific methods involved, though many theories do exist (including, but not limited to aliens.) What the evidence does show, however, is that the pyramids were built by peasants who were fed, housed and paid while their fields were submerged during the annual flooding of the Nile.

During the time of the old kingdom, previously autonomous and independent portions of Egypt fell under the sole ruler of the pharaoh. This led to some perks, but also placed a much greater deal of responsibility on the pharaoh as he or she would then have to assume the duties which would previously have been performed by the regional governors.

In 2495 BC began the fifth dynasty. This would be a dynasty where pyramids were still constructed to a point, but they were not nearly on such a grand scale as those of Sneferu and Khufu. This period did not see cessation of all impressive buildings, however. During the fifth dynasty, temples to Ra, the sun god and chief deity of Egypt were constructed and cults of Ra became more and more prominent.

The period of the fifth dynasty saw a large increase in trade with merchants travelling not only along the Nile, but over the Mediterranean Sea as well. This was one of the important changes during the fifth dynasty that likely affected the future of the old kingdom.

By the sixth dynasty, the nobles of Egypt began to grow richer; in some cases, even moreso than the king. It is theorized that this actually happened due to the pharaoh's levying a lighter tax burden on the wealthier and more favored individuals of the kingdom. This process led to super-wealthy nobility, and an increasingly pocket-poor state. Evidence of this can be witnessed in the grandiose tombs of the nobility and the lesser tombs of the pharaohs during this period.

Between the increase in trade and regional affluence, the power of the pharaohs diminished in favor of local leaders known as nomarchs. Nomarchs were rulers of their respective regions, and power was actually given to them, in most cases, by the pharaoh himself in order to make wider rule of all of Egypt more efficient. As time went on, however, these nomarchs formed their own dynasties independent of the pharaoh bloodline and thus led to a tumultuous sixth dynasty.

Things came to a head when Pepi II was pharaoh. He lived and ruled an unusually long time. This caused many issues, including Pepi II outliving his heirs. The bloodline of the pharaohs was lost, and within a short amount of time, unrest and disorder swept through the land. The nail in the coffin where the sixth dynasty and the old kingdom itself finally came effectively to an end was a period of lower flood-levels from the Nile. This left the crops sparse, the people hungry and the temperament of the people irritable to say the very least.

It wasn't until this all-encompassing power of the pharaoh started to languish that the old kingdom came to an end.

CHAPTER 10

Collapse and Rebirth

The time of the first intermediate period was a time marred by conflict in Egypt. The power of the pharaohs had become weakened to the point that they were often ineffective against the regional leaders, the nomarchs. The nomarchs wielded power over the forty-two major cities, or nomes, and as the power of the pharaohs became ever more diminished, these rulers stepped in the fill the gaps.

The first intermediate period was likely not due to a shift in power, but a shift in water. The flooding of the Nile, such a crucial yearly event, had been especially low. Crops were lost and famine was widespread.

Although the power of the pharaohs was diminished, it wasn't gone completely. The seventh through tenth dynasties were during this time, and part of the eleventh dynasty was also during this period.

Not too much is known of the seventh and eighth dynasties, however, it is generally regarded that the seventh dynasty consisted of oligarchical rule, that is, rule by a few elite individuals as opposed to a kingship. It was also written by a historian and priest Manetho that there was at one point seventy kings within seventy days, however, this is commonly dismissed as hyperbole. A couple of likely explanations of this claim are that kingship was heavily disputed and no king held pharaohship for long. Another possibility is that, due to the rise of feuding power structures within Egypt, there were more than one king at a time who either ruled a portion of the land, or claimed to be ruler of all Egypt. The truth of the matter is that although many claimed power during this period, Egypt was, for all intents and purposes, anarchic.

Unfortunately, apart from Manetho, who was from a much later period of time, during the Greek rule of Egypt, there is precious little preserved about the first intermediate period. Not only that, we do not have, at least to our present knowledge, the actual works from Manetho's hands. All that we have of his writings are from other historians who must have had some knowledge or experience with Manetho's writings, at least enough that they referenced them. The problem here is that we don't know what would have been Manetho's word, and what would have been the word of the later historians.

The eighth dynasty, like those before it, ruled from Memphis. It's often postulated that these rulers claimed heirship due to the bloodline of the sixth dynasty which they claimed to have possessed, however, not much is known about this dynasty.

The ninth dynasty was the first to rule from outside of Memphis. These rulers affected their control from Herakleopolis (a Greek name, given to this city much later, meaning "City of Hercules." It's possible that the ninth dynasty saw a reunification of Egypt; however, this did not stand for long. The first king of this dynasty was said to have been of choleric temperament and took out his aggression on the people of Egypt.

During the first intermediate period, power was more or less split between Thebes and Memphis, although the Herakleopolitan rulers did see a great increase in power during this time. Due to the schism, there are relatively distinct architecture and artistic influences depending on the region from whence they came.

One of the most important things regarding the art referring to this period lies in the "literature" around the beginning of the middle kingdom. Much of this literature was in the form of laments, or lamentations. Lamentations are cries, writings, basically some form of expression where the person lamenting is trying to express their sadness or loss of hope. As these lamentations are generally regarded as either fictional or unreliable accounts of history, it's difficult to tell where actual events stop and the imagination of the writer or scribe begins, however, from these, we can deduce some things about the first intermediate period.

One of the lamentations suggests that Egypt was invaded by foreigners. This would have been the first known instance of an invasion by a faction outside of Egypt itself (although it would be far from the last.) Whether it was a military invasion, immigration or happened at all is uncertain, but the scribe goes on to suggest that the old order of things within Egypt had more or less been dissolved. Slave girls, the writer of this lamentation would say, were decked out in gold and other precious metals and jewels. By this can be extrapolated that the old order of the king or pharaoh having the most, then the nobles having much, etc. on down the line, was upset, and the Egyptians were not a people geared toward change.

This particular lamentation also alludes to many instances of grave-robbing and class warfare, particularly in the guise of attack of the nobles and the wealthy by the commoners. Other lamentations are more focused on spiritual ideals, but all seem to describe a yearning to return to the times of glory under Sneferu, the original builder of pyramids. Whether this longing had anything to do with the rise of the middle kingdom or not is uncertain, however, all sources suggest a great deal of unrest and unhappiness during this period between 2181 and 2040 B.C.

So much grave-robbing happened during the first intermediate period, in fact, that it wasn't just the tombs of the commoners or the nobility that were robbed; targets also included the great pyramids of Giza. One can only imagine what treasures of history may have been found in Khufu's pyramid, or Sneferu's, or any one of countless other sites looted during this time. Unfortunately, however, the greed and disorder of the time led to the loss of whatever artifacts may have been found. In fact, not only were things normally considered to be valuables taken, but in a lot of cases, the sarcophagi, body included, were removed.

But that was about to change.

This isn't to say that all of the power was consolidated with the pharaoh, in fact, a great deal of the regional leadership would come from local governors. However, these governors would come to be united under the pharaoh. It wasn't an easy process at first. The pharaoh had to actually ask these governors to send men for the purpose of army-building, however, it wouldn't be long until the pharaohs yielded the kind of power that they had during the old kingdom.

The eleventh dynasty is marked by a great deal of struggle for these kings to gain this power and unification. It is with the eleventh dynasty that rule begins from the city of Thebes. One of the interesting things about both dynasties of the middle kingdom is that many of the leaders had the same name or, more accurately, their names began with the same word. In the eleventh dynasty, the name was Intef.

This has made tracing the history of this period a bit difficult at times, as papyri and tablets recovered are often degraded or fragmented. This is such a problem in that often times the full name of the pharaoh is not present, and thus it can be difficult to say with certainty from these sources, exactly which king did what. Some things are known though.

There was a progression from the first king Intef, whose full name was Intef Sehertawi (or Seher-towi, Seher-tawi, etc.) which roughly translates to "Causing Peace Between Two Lands." This is a reference to the fragmented Egypt, and although this king was far from pharaoh of all Egypt, it begins to signify an intention toward reunification and consolidation of power. Although his name inferred a bringer of peace or at least pacification, Sehertawi began waging war against the leaders of the north, which did lead to a greater amount of control to the dynastic rulers of Thebes.

After Intef Sehertawi came Intef Wahankh, or "Established in Life." Wahankh (or Wah-Ankh) consolidated the Upper Kingdom under his rule and battled with the rulers of the north for greater control of Egypt. This finally ended with Wahankh gaining control of the important city of Abydos. Apart from this, not much is known about Intef Wahankh, other than the fact that he was a great lover of his dogs. In 1860, a stelé was found of this king whose funerary stelé had five dogs on it, presumably his.

It was with Intef Nakht Neb Tep Nefer (or Nakht-nebtepnefer,) or "beautiful and mighty lord," that a much larger effort was made in order to fully reunify the Upper and Lower Kingdoms whose close ties had been severed, or at least frayed, near the end of the old kingdom into the first intermediate period. He led a military expedition from Thebes in the south, or the Upper Kingdom against the people of the north, the Lower Kingdom.

The Lower Kingdom was still under the rule of the tenth dynasty of the Herakleopolitan rulers (not to be confused with the tenth dynasty of Egypt which had since passed) and, like most rulers the world has known, they weren't very willing to give up their power without a fight, and a fight is exactly what they gave. Many battles were fought and would continue to be fought between the Theban kings of the south and the Herakleopolitan kings of the north.

CHAPTER 11

Pharaohs and the Middle Kingdom

It was during the eleventh dynasty that Egypt would finally become stable and united under one rule. It was during the reign of Mentuhotep II that the bickering and disjunct powers would become consolidated and the rule of Egypt would rest once more into the hands of the pharaoh. The middle kingdom would last from 2134 to 1782 B.C.

The middle kingdom came into being at or around the thirty-ninth year of Mentuhotep II's rule. Mentuhotep II's Horus name was Se-ankh-ib-towi, or "Making the Heart of the Two Lands Alive/To Live." There is debate as to whether Mentuhotep II was or wasn't the son of the last Intef, Intef Nakhtnebtepnefer, but it is certain that his rule would bring a great change to Egypt.

It was his mission to complete the intention of his forefathers and bring the land of Lower Egypt under his control and thus unify the country once more under a single ruler. He sent a military campaign against the Herakleopolitans during a revolt in one of the nomes to the north.

Much of what we know about Mentuhotep comes from his burial site. It was a departure from the burial sites of previous kings in many ways, although in the center did stand a small pyramid. Much of the actual structure of the mortuary temple is gone or in ruin today, however, some things survived which give us an insight into the times.

For instance there is a mass grave holding sixty or more mummified young men was discovered. These men were not children, but they were young, probably twenties to thirties, and they showed signs of being killed in battle. From this, we can extrapolate some of the violence and warfare which occurred during the battles for reunification under Mentuhotep's rule.

Along with this, we see caskets in the harem section of the complex which housed not only the mummified remains of those who died around this time, but spells and incantations to assist the dead in making their way to the land of the dead, spells intending to help these people be resurrected on the other side. At the end of the fifth dynasty, the pharaoh Unas was the first to have ritual texts in his pyramid chamber, but these beliefs were expanding to include incantations written out inside of the sarcophagus. This speaks to an even more important sense of religion during the beginning of the middle kingdom than was apparent in the old.

Mentuhotep II was the first pharaoh in quite a while to identify himself as a god among men. He wore a headdress of two gods, Min and Amun (or Amoun.) During the eleventh dynasty, Amun would become the god of Thebes, or the patron god of Thebes. Amun was the god of the wind and, during much of Egypt's history, the king of the gods.

The middle kingdom was a time of great expansion. Military outposts rose up in various parts of Egypt's spreading area of influence. As the borders of Egypt expanded, so did the power of the pharaohs. Although the middle kingdom only saw two dynasties (the eleventh and twelfth,) it was a time of great power and growth for not only the pharaohs, but for the people of Egypt as well.

When Mentuhotep II died after a reign of over fifty years, kingship passed on to his son, Mentuhotep III or Mentuhotep Se-Ankh-Ka-Re. It was with Mentuhotep III that more expeditions would be undertaken and fortresses built. These forts were often built larger than necessary for purposes of intimidation. The power of Egypt was back, and the pharaohs wanted their enemies to know it.

Although Mentuhotep III would only reign for twelve years, much can be extrapolated about the state of the pharaohs during this time. One of the most profound indications that the pharaoh's power was growing to a point that hadn't been seen since before the first intermediate period was the expedition to the Wadi Hammamat.

The goal of this expedition was to bring back fine, black stone, gum, perfume and incense. Without some context, this may sound like a simple task and a simple journey, but the expedition to the land of Wadi Hammamat was over arid deserts, over which, the 3,000 men who made the journey not only drove out marauders, but dug twelve individual wells in order to sustain the men. Along with this, it is said that each of the men would carry two jugs of water, both for his own use; and that pack animals, most likely donkeys, carried containers full of extra sandals, due to the short life of footwear under these conditions. Such an expedition hadn't been attempted since the old kingdom, and it was quite the statement of the growing power of the pharaoh.

After Mentuhotep III came Mentuhotep IV, or Neb-Towi-Re (or Nebtawire, Neb-Tawi-Re, etc.) whose name meant something to the effect of, "Re is the lord of the two lands." As if the expedition of 3,000 men by his father wasn't enough, Mentuhotep IV sent another expedition to Wadi Hammamat, only this time, he more than tripled the number of men to 10,000.

Of the last king of the eleventh dynasty, Mentuhotep IV, not much else is known. In fact, other than inscriptions in the Wadi Hammamat regarding the expedition of the 10,000 men, the histories of the time regarded the seven years when Mentuhotep would have been pharaoh as seven empty years. It is, however, likely that his vizier (an advisor, esp. to royalty) succeeded him as pharaoh.

The history of Menetho and the Turin King List disagree as to exactly how many pharaohs ruled over the eleventh dynasty of Egypt. The Turin King List is one of many such lists created to make tracking the progression of time throughout the dynasties. As mentioned in an earlier chapter, before these king lists, dates were recorded as years of a particular pharaoh's rule (i.e. third year of Khufu, etc.) The problem with this was that as time went on, it wasn't always clear who ruled at what point in time and for how long. This was largely (though not completely) rectified through use of various king lists.

Mentuhotep's vizier was named Amenemhet (or Amenemhet.) The first pharaoh of the twelfth dynasty bore this same name. While it is possible that the ruler Amenemhet I, first king of the twelfth dynasty, used the name as a reference to the vizier, this possibility is slim, and it's generally postulated that Amenemhet I was, in fact the vizier to the last Mentuhoteps. This suggests that the previous bloodline may have been overthrown with Amenemhet I taking the throne as usurper (he ruled between 1991 and 1962 B.C.,) and some evidence may suggest a form of internal conflict during this period, however this is unconfirmed.

What is quite interesting in regard to Amenemhet is that he did not have royal blood. Although he wasn't a commoner in the sense that he worked the fields in order to sustain his living, he had no direct claim to kingship. This may also strengthen the case of usurpation. In a papyrus that Amenemhet is said to have commissioned, he claims that he was destined to be king.

This particular prophecy is notable as it was claimed to have been written at some point during the old kingdom, however, all indications show that it would have been during Amenemhet I's time. This seems to be one of the earliest (if not the earliest) uses of propaganda by a political leader.

Like the kings of the previous dynasty, he had a Horus name. This name was Weham-mswe, or "Repeater of births," or "Repetition of birth." It is postulated that Amenemhet used this name to signify a period of regrowth and further reunification of the land. Although the pharaohs of the previous dynasty were credited with reuniting Egypt, which, to a certain degree, they did, it was particularly during the twelfth dynasty that this reunification found an increase in strength and stability.

Amenemhet would move the capitol of Egypt yet again. This time from Thebes, well in the south, to a location which is somewhat vague to us today; but somewhere in the Faiyum region. This capitol was called Amenemhet-itj-tawy, or "Amenemhet, seizer/binder of the two lands." The name of this city would tell the people of Egypt that unification had happened, and was to stay that way under his rule and that of his dynasty.

The tombs of this period were much more intricate than those of the eleventh dynasty and much more elaborate than those of the first intermediate period. Amenemhet himself commissioned a pyramid of his own. It didn't have the scale or the grandeur of the pyramids of Khufu or Sneferu, however, it did utilize a traditional entrance. That is, the entrance faced the North Star. This likely symbolized that just as the North Star was unmoving in the night-sky, so would the pharaoh be constant and eternal.

Another mark of the twelfth dynasty is that the artisans, who had lost much of their skill by the time the eleventh dynasty came along, began to create much more intricate statues, sculptures and other works, the likes of which are much more familiar to us today.

Before his death, Amenemhet did something which was unusual, and possibly entirely new for the pharaohs of Egypt. Approximately ten years before his death, he made his son coregent or co-ruler of Egypt. The reason behind this seems to hearken back to the collapse of the old kingdom when Pepi, the last of the old kingdom's pharaohs, died without a viable heir to the throne.

While sources are uncertain, it appears that Amenemhet may have been assassinated. This makes the "training," if you will, of his son and heir, Senusret I particularly important. Not only was the new pharaoh of the royal bloodline, he was also very well-prepared to be king. This custom of exalting one's heir while the pharaoh was still alive and at rule would continue on even through the new kingdom.

Senusret I, who reigned from about 1971-1926 B.C., carried on the fortification of Egypt and expansion into other areas, specifically the land of Kush (later Nubia, present day Sudan.) Here he built massive fortresses to not only instill his presence, but to preserve it as well. The journey to the land of Kush was primarily to gain more resources. He also led expeditions into the Wadi Hammamat to collect materials for buildings, tombs, etc.

One of the sites that would receive the greatest amount of attention during this time was called Heliopolis (a later Greek name meaning "City of the Sun.") Heliopolis was the home of the sun cult or cult of Ra (or Re.) In the area of Heliopolis, still stands one of the obelisks from Sesostris's time. This obelisk is sixty-seven feet tall and weighs in at an impressive 120 tons. Apart from Heliopolis itself, many other architectural wonders would be created including obelisks, temples, chapels, tombs and even a pyramid for Sesostris himself.

Sesostris would follow in his father's footsteps in two ways, one, he utilized propaganda to declare himself the rightful ruler and heir of Amenemhet, his father. This papyrus is purported to be Amenemhet's advice to his son regarding how to rule the kingdom. What makes it particularly obvious that Amenemhet couldn't have written this, was that it references his own murder. While they pharaohs were considered gods, and the papyrus doesn't specifically mention the killing itself, it does give an idea of the events which possibly led to Amenemhet's demise in 1962 B.C.

The other thing that Sesostris did like his father was he had his own son made coregent of Egypt. His son was named Amenemhet II after his grandfather, the father of Sesostris and the first pharaoh of the twelfth dynasty.

Although Amenemhet II would rule for a reasonably long time (1929-1895) very little is known about him. It is known that he sent an expedition to Wadi Hammamat, constructed a white pyramid, and that the powers of Egypt were wide-reaching. In fact, even in areas of the Middle East, such as Lebanon have been excavated which have shown trade-goods bearing the name of Amenemhet II. The period of Amenemhet II's rule was marked largely by a prolific amount of international trade.

Sesostris II (ruled 1897-1878 B.C. although the length of his reign is heavily disputed) was made coregent by his father Amenemhet II, and would soon rule over the land. One thing particularly notable about Sesostris II is that he was much more focused on peace between nearby lands than many of his predecessors. During his reign, we see increased stability and inspection and rebuilding of fortresses. His power was more consolidated and he took steps to ensure its continuation through such means.

Diplomatic relations with Syria and Palestine were continued and strengthened. Along with this, he focused a great deal on the Faiyum region, a depression or oasis near the area of Cairo. He planned and carried out massive irrigation projects through the Faiyum area.

His son was Sesostris III. Sesostris III was an enormous man by the standards of ancient Egypt, and quite tall by our standards today at 6' 6". His reign saw a push to occupy more lands in Nubia, the construction of a canal to bypass the first cataract on the Nile (section of river rapids or waterfall) and, although he was a very militaristic leader, especially in the early to midpoint of his reign, these very campaigns would ensure a level of peace and prosperity.

The nomarchs during this time had grown again in and affluence, but Sesostris III's reign actually saw a shift in power from the regional nomarchs to the pharaoh in a way that belied the wealth of the nomarchs.

With Amenemhet III, a shift in tradition occurred. Like his father, statues depicting him were different from those in the past. The pharaoh was depicted as having a weary expression. One of the possible reasons for this can be found in Amenemhet's pyramid.

Amenemhet III's pyramid was constructed in a way to deter, probably originally to prevent, grave robbing. All of the pyramids previous to Amenemhet III's had entrances on the north side, pointing toward the North Star. Amenemhet III's, however, had an entrance on the south side. While it was still eventually robbed, it made location of the entrance much more difficult for archaeologists to find as it was oriented on the opposite side of what these investigators were used to. In fact, when the pyramid was first accessed, it was entered through digging and removing stones from the top.

The inside of this pyramid also offered false passageways or dead ends: likely also to deter grave robbers from reaching the king's chamber.

Another thing that Amenemhet did was continue trying to connect the waters of the Nile with the Faiyum area. He not only expanded the canal, but also constructed a dam. Work on this area which would come to be known as Lake Moeris wouldn't be finished until his son, Amenemhet IV.

Amenemhet IV built the only temple from the middle kingdom period which survives to a reasonable degree today, although even this temple in the Faiyum area is largely in ruin. Amenemhet is often referred to as the last real king of the middle kingdom.

After Amenemhet IV, the next pharaoh was a woman, likely his step-sister or aunt, though it is theorized that she may have been his wife. Her name was Sobeknefru.

Precious little is known about the rule of Sobeknefru, other than it was after her short reign that the political structure of Egypt would collapse and enter into the second intermediate period.

CHAPTER 12

Moving Toward the New Kingdom

The second intermediate period would be a time of weakening pharaotic power, it would be a time of invasion and occupation, and it would eventually see Egypt rising up again. As you look through various other great civilizations throughout the world and throughout history, very seldom do you see a civilization return from collapse, much less twice. This would be, however, exactly what happened in Egypt.

The second intermediate period and the collapse of the power structure in Egypt didn't happen overnight. What we can see though, looking at the history of this time is a continual weakening of the pharaohs' power and influence.

With the thirteenth dynasty, of which little is known about, there are still some temples, pyramids and sculptures constructed. This shows that things didn't just collapse quickly into anarchy like the first intermediate period is thought to have done, however, there is a distinct weakening of the power of the pharaohs and the reach of Egypt.

The middle period had lasted from 2055-1650 (or 2125-1782 depending on source) B.C., and had seen a regrowth and expansion that hadn't been conceptualized since the old kingdom. However, things start to fail.

The fourteenth dynasty moved the capitol from the Faiyum region to the area of the Nile delta to the north. This change in location shows that the fourteenth dynasty may have been more concerned with invasion from the north, from the Mediterranean Sea. It could also suggest that these rulers had no actual claim to heirship, although this is uncertain at best.

It was with the fifteenth dynasty that everything would change. The fifteenth dynasty was made up of Hyksos. Hyksos used to be translated as "shepherd kings." However, in more recent years, it has been more commonly accepted as meaning "foreign kings." It's uncertain exactly who these people were, although it's likely that they came from Palestine and/or Syria.

The other perplexing thing about the Hyksos is that we're not entirely certain whether they took power as invaders through military action, or whether they were merely immigrants and the descendants of immigrants who seized power peacefully having lived in Egypt for an elongated period of time.

We do know that the Hyksos had begun to take power during the middle kingdom in the area of the delta, a region of Egypt where immigrants and foreigners were much more commonplace. The capitol was now at Avaris in the north, and this dynasty did not have complete control of the land.

Here we see the real fissures in what had been a very productive and unified middle kingdom. In fact, it would be this disjunction of power that would result in the rise of the sixteenth dynasty.

The sixteenth dynasty of Egypt probably ruled from Thebes, although there are conflicting accounts. This dynasty did not last very long and was plagued by battles against the surviving fifteenth dynasty to the north. There were small times of peace, but the rulers of the fifteenth dynasty had many victories in the south, including the eventual conquering of the city of Thebes. This dynasty is often not considered to have actual ruling power as the fifteenth dynasty in the north continued until the rise of the seventeenth dynasty.

As if two dynasties going at the same time weren't bad enough for the already fractured Egypt, discoveries in the last twenty years or so have shown that there were also dynastic rulers in Abydos during the same time as the fifteenth and sixteenth dynasties. It is obvious that this period was a time of enormous fragmentation of power, near constant conflict between these powers and an Egypt which would not see unification for quite some time.

It's with the seventeenth dynasty that things finally start to come together for the Egyptians again. During the time just before the rise of the seventeenth dynasty, the Hyksos of the fifteenth dynasty were still at rule in the north but, apart from putting down the warring faction of the sixteenth dynasty, they generally preferred to stay up north. The city of Thebes at this time was ruled by princes, Theban princes. It was from these princes that the seventeenth dynasty would rise.

There is a papyrus which, though largely a work of fiction, gives us an idea of what happened between the Hyksos of the fifteenth dynasty and the Theban princes of the seventeenth. The story goes that the King Apophis of the Hyksos sent a missive to Sekhemre-Heruhirmaat Intef, the Theban who would become the first pharaoh of the seventeenth dynasty. These cities were somewhere around five-hundred miles apart, yet King Aphophis complained that the hippopotamuses in Sekhemre's area were keeping him from sleeping. In the fiction, Sekhemre's then leads a bunch of troops against the petulant king.

While this version is beyond unlikely, it is true that Sekhemre would lead a campaign against Pharaoh Apophis in the north. This campaign wasn't successful, however the future campaigns of his descendants would be.

These pharaohs continued their campaign against the Hyksos of Lower Egypt, having increased success in their campaigns, but it wasn't until Ahmose I that the Hyksos were finally driven out and the eighteenth dynasty, and thus the new kingdom, began.

CHAPTER 13

The New Kingdom Flourishes

With the advent of the eighteenth dynasty, the Hyksos had been chased out of Egypt and the new kingdom (approx. 1550-1077 B.C.) was established. This wasn't enough for Ahmose, however, as he pursued the Hyksos and captured many settlements outside of Egypt along the way. He also reinforced the western border. This was to deter and protect against another Hyksos invasion, or an invasion of the Hyksos allies. During this time, a permanent army was established. This would have a great impact on the new kingdom.

When Ahmose finally returned to rule as the sole pharaoh of Egypt, Thebes was officially established as the capitol of Egypt. Egypt, during the second intermediate period and the fifteenth dynasty, had a couple of different capitols as the country was not unified as it once was: one at Thebes and one in the north. Ahmose quickly established this new capitol and began his reign by building monuments to his mother and grandmother. It would be a mark of the new kingdom that women were held in much higher regard.

Ahmose would not cease his military campaigns. After the expulsion of the Hyksos, he set his sights on Nubia. Along with having valuable resources, Nubian archers (often referred to as bowmen) were a threat that Ahmose did not want to ignore. Whether there were any indications of planned campaigns by the Nubians against the Egyptians is speculative and doubtful. What we do know is that the campaign was a success for the Egyptians.

Here it is interesting to note the way that Egyptians would count the number of men they had killed in battle. The Egyptians liked to keep track of everything of a battle (with the exception of battles they lost which were generally not mentioned.) To that end, they would bring along scribes to keep track of the spoils of victory and the amount of men slain.

The way that the scribes would count the numbers of enemy dead is that the soldiers would cut off the right hand of the slain enemy and toss them in a pile in the center of the battlefield. This way, the scribe could make an accurate (or reasonably accurate) count of the number of men slain. It wasn't uncommon for warriors to brag, boast and in some instances be rewarded for the number of hands that they took.

After a long and successful rule in which Ahmose I gave his wife a title translating to "wife of a god," the rule of Egypt would pass to his son Amenhotep I.

Amenhotep I, like his father was a warlike pharaoh. He continued to campaign against the Nubians and, according to one source, in a massive battle, he either killed or made them captives. None were said to have escaped. The scale of this is probably a reference to those who were in the battle and not the Nubians as a whole, but we do see quite a few captives taken at this time.

The army during this point in time was very well established. Training started young with some trainees beginning as young as age five. The training consisted of a number of things. In order to demoralize recruits and thus make them more suggestible to orders and training, recruits were given a intense beating. After this, they would undergo many other training programs including sword fighting, throwing knives, using sandbags to lift weights, boxing, wrestling, bow and arrow training and chariot riding. Although formal military service didn't begin until age twenty, many Egyptians began their path in the military at a very young age.

Unlike times past when Egypt didn't have a standing army, this army was well-trained, disciplined and most importantly for the recruits, they could work their way up the ranks. This was a big deal for commoners who had previously been more or less stuck in their station before the new kingdom, but it had a profound impact on the number of recruits who were willing to join and the morale of the army as a whole.

One of the more interesting things about Amenhotep I is that he was the first pharaoh in the known history of Egypt to have a separation between his mortuary temple and his tomb. This was unique in that pharaohs before him had both their tomb and their temple quite close to one another, so that their spirits would be close to the offerings of food, drinks, etc. that the priests would bring to the temple. It's likely that Amenhotep did this to discourage grave-robbing.

When Amenhotep I died, he did not have a male heir. This being the case, it was Thutmose I, a commoner who married the daughter of King and Queen Ahmose Nefertari. It was due to this marriage that he was able to take the throne. Because Amenhotep didn't have a son, the succession was based off of who would marry and bear children of the "purest" royal blood. Incest was common among the pharaohs and their queens during Ancient Egypt, much like it would be for millennia afterward in other monarchist societies. The reason for this was the preservation of the royal blood. Although Thutmose did not himself have royal blood, due to his marriage with the daughter of Ahmose, he was close enough.

Like his predecessors he entered Nubia in order to gain resources and exert his power, however, he went much farther down the Nile than those who came before him. One of the men who joined his was named Ahmose, son of Ebana (not to be confused with pharaoh Ahmose.) Ahmose, son of Ebana had campaigned with two previous pharaohs by this time, Ahmose I (1549 - 1524) and Amenhotep I (1524 - 1503.)

By this point in his life, Ahmose, son of Ebana would have been well into his fifties, and the journey was perilous. Regardless, with Ahmose, son of Ebana at his side, Thutmose I would conquer two of the Nubian tribes and also a group of Bedouins (people of the desert.) As if that wasn't a large enough display of power, he also erected an enormous stelé, claiming the fifth cataract (up until then, well into Nubian territory) as the southern border of the land of Egypt. And, just for good measure, he pinned the body of a Nubian leader upside down and dead from the prow of his ship. The body would remain there until he returned to Thebes.

Thutmose I was far from finished though. He and his army would continue on and march far north to Mesopotamia, conquering as they went. When he reached his destination, he erected a large stelé here as well, claiming this as the northern border of Egypt.

At his death, Thutmose would be the first pharaoh to be buried in the Valley of the Kings on the west bank of the Nile near Thebes. This would come to be a trend among future pharaohs. The Valley of the Kings became popular as a burial site due to several factors that it was so arid and barren (it still is to this day) that neither Thutmose I or those who would follow him would have to worry about settlements cropping up around the site. Another reason is that the top of the mountain in the area is a natural pyramid-like point. This would have been appealing as a reference to the incredible monuments of the past. Last, but not least, is the fact that there is only one way in or out of this area. That would have been much easier to guard. Although this didn't entirely deter grave-robbers, it went a long way to preserving many of the artifacts that we have today.

Upon Thutmose's death, though he had fathered three sons and two daughters, all but one daughter had died. Her name was Hatshepsut. She would have been only twelve years (or so) at the time of her father's death, but with no other heirs with pure royal blood, it came to one of Thutmose's sons from a concurrent marriage, also named Thutmose, to marry Hatshepsut and become pharaoh.

In Egypt, it was common for the pharaoh to have multiple wives, but there was a structure to this. The pharaoh would have one "great wife," this would be the woman from whom the first heirs would be chosen. These were the heirs thought to be of purest blood. The pharaoh also had other wives. These wives were still highly regarded within the house, but there was only ever one great wife. If there was no viable heir from the union with the great wife, the heir would then be chosen from among the children of these wives. There were also consorts of the pharaoh. These wives were by no means disrespected, in fact, they were highly revered. It was from the consorts that the pharaoh's heir would come should no viable heir be chosen from the great wife's children (if she had any) or the wives' children (if they had any.) Thutmose II would have been the son of one of Thutmose I's wives, Mutnofret.

Thutmose II was married to Hatshepsut for twenty years until his death. When he died, the question came again, "Who is going to be pharaoh?" Thutmose II had a son by another woman. He was Thutmose III. He would have been Hatshepsut's step-son and, due to the fact that Thutmose II was her half-brother, Thutmose III would have also been her nephew. He would become one of the most remarkable pharaohs of all Egypt's history.

Before Thutmose III could take power though, he had to grow up. He would have been about six or seven years old at this time. Therefore, Hatshepsut became regent. That is, acting pharaoh until Thutmose III grew to the proper age. At one point, however, Hatshepsut would declare herself king. She would be pharaoh and even went so far as to don the "false beard of authority" which the pharaohs are often seen wearing in their kas or other depictions.

Hatshepsut's reign would be a remarkable one. She would build an incredible monument which still stands today. It would depict numerous things, but largely it would depict an expedition into the land of Punt (location still unknown,) that she sent. The drawings inside Hatshepsut's monument would be the first accurate depiction of the area that was visited. Hatshepsut also instituted the first zoo in the history of the world. The expedition to Punt would return with many treasures including animals, incense and, notably, trees from which the incense was made. These were brought back to Thebes and planted.

She would also erect four obelisks on the east bank of Thebes at Karnack temple. One of the most interesting things that Hatshepsut had included inside her monument was that of her divine birth. This was by no means a new custom. Most pharaohs, at least of the time, would depict their "divine birth" in the very same way (that of being molded on a potter's wheel) by the god Khnum, the god who created all humans according the ancient Egyptians. Whether it was a mistake of those who did the inscriptions, or something that Hatshepsut decided herself, she was depicted (with her ka, as was always present in such hieroglyphs) as being formed a male. Although many of the aspects of Hatshepsut's reign could be misconstrued that she was attempting to masquerade as a man, this was not the case. She was a proud woman, and referred to herself as "the female/woman falcon."

Also, according to the walls of the monument, the god Amun came to Hatshepsut's mother, Ahmose, in her husband's form. Ahmose then lied with the god and became pregnant with Hatshepsut. This was the mythos created to signify her right to rule as pharaoh.

Hatshepsut also erected two tombs for herself. One was built as the tomb of the Queen of Egypt, which she had been for some time, however, the one which she favored and to which she committed her earthly remains was in the Valley of the Kings.

Though Thutmose III would grow to adulthood during Hatshepsut's continued reign, she remained pharaoh for the remainder of her life. When Thutmose III finally became pharaoh, a little more of the story comes out in what he does regarding the places in which Hatshepsut's name is carved. He removes her name entirely. After removing her name, he adds in the names of his forefathers, Thutmose I, Thutmose II and, in some cases, his own name. Where this begins to grow a bit clearer is that in a couple of places, Hatshepsut is depicted, standing in front of Thutmose III. He had grown to adulthood a while before the end of Hatshepsut's reign, however, it seems that she may have used her influence as pharaoh to keep him from taking power until her death. This seems to be the reason behind Thutmose attempting to erase her name from history; however, evidence shows that this may not actually have been done out of spite. It is more than likely that the Egyptians of the time simply wanted to remove record of a woman being pharaoh. Regardless of how it happened, Hatshepsut was one of the most influential pharaohs of all ancient Egypt.

Thutmose III is most widely regarded as the most successful warlike pharaoh of ancient Egypt. He would send forth many campaigns to various parts of the nearby world. It's likely that while Hatshepsut was ruling, he was in the military being trained, learning strategy and developing the skills that would make him such a successful warlord.

His first campaign was to Megiddo. While Hatshepsut was pharaoh, she led few military campaigns, and the Syrro-Palestine (area of modern-day Syria and Palestine) people had stopped paying their tribute to Egypt for the most part. This was tolerated under Hatshepsut's rule, but as the Syrro-Palestinians began to grow more independent, Thutmose III decided that something would have to be done.

He led his army through a narrow valley, surprising the army of Megiddo well outside the city walls and utterly dominating them in combat. The army of

Megiddo retreated into the city and was able to re-group. Because the Egyptians were busier plundering the fallen enemies than they were with finishing the job against their living enemies, they had to lay siege to the city of Megiddo for a period of seven months. After the long siege, the walls of Megiddo finally fell and Thutmose III took the city.

The next eighteen years would see return trips to Syrro-Palestine to "remind" the Syrians of their duty to send tribute to Egypt. He would also campaign to Phoenician coastal outposts which were changed into Egyptian bases. He would also take Kadesh and other cities in and around the Bekaa region and also Mitanni. Thutmose III would die in 1425 B.C.

Thutmose III's successor was Amenhotep II. He would preserve the expanded kingdom that his father had built, however, during his reign came a sort of peace between Egypt and Syrro-Palestine.

Amenhotep II's successor was Thutmose IV. Thutmose IV wasn't intended to be the heir to the throne, how-ever it is likely that he usurped power by stepping in front of his brother. He would commission what is called "The Dream Stelé," a move that would attempt to justify why he, and not his older brother would take the throne. Thutmose IV is most well-known for restoring the Sphinx.

Under Thutmose IV's son, Amenhotep III, pharaoh after his father's death in 1391 B.C., Egypt would see an age of prosperity and artistic accomplishment. Of all of the pharaohs throughout the history of ancient Egypt, more statues of Amenhotep III survive today than any other. It was in his son, however, that many historians are more interested.

Amenhotep III's son was named Amenhotep IV. Many people aren't familiar with the name Amenhotep IV. That's because only a few years into his reign, he changed his name to Akhenaten.

Akhenaten (reigned 1351–1334 B.C.) is known best for turning his back on the religion of Egypt in a big way. The Egyptians had been polytheistic (belief in more than one god) for as long as history has records, however, Akenaten instituted worship of the sun-disk, called Aten. In fact, the name Akhenaten means "Effective/Effectual for Aten." The thing is, only he and his family were actually allowed to worship Aten. The rest of Egypt was meant to worship him. This makes his change not to monotheism, rather to a ditheistic religion. Akhenaten is also well known because of his wife, Nefertiti.

Nefertiti is somewhat an enigma as it seems that nobody knows where she came from. There are theories as to her heritage, but these are unconfirmed. Just as mysteriously as she came into the picture, so would she fade back out of it. However, she has been immortalized in the now iconic bust that was made of her.

This period of the new kingdom would come to be known as the Amarna period, due to the advent of Akhenaten's city of the same name. Although this was a primary goal, from what we know, of his leadership, this change would not last.

There is some dispute as to who came next. The records of this period are largely destroyed by the future kings who would reinstitute the full pantheon of Egyptian gods.

Both of Akhenaten's possible successors also subscribed to the Amarna principle. One of them was named Smenkhkare. Not much is known of Smenkhkare, largely due to the fact that future pharaohs would seek to destroy evidence of the Armana period as referenced above.

The other possible successor was named Neferneferuaten. It's debated whether Neferneferuaten was a man or a woman, or was actually Nefertiti or Smenkhkare. What is known is who came next.

King Tut, as he's commonly referred to in colloquial conversation today was the young Pharaoh Tutankhamen. Tutankhamen was the son of Akhenaten. The way that we know this with such certainty is that the DNA of both Akhenaten and Tut were tested against each other and Tutankhamen was found to be the son.

Pharaoh Tutankhamen is, quite honestly, best known due to the fact that his tomb was relatively intact when it was discovered. His burial mask has become iconic for ancient Egypt, although Tut would not have been pharaoh for very long, likely nine years. This rule would have been from the age of nine to the age of eighteen, the time of his death (1323 B.C.)

Rumors persisted for quite a while, and sometimes to this day, about the "curse of King Tut's tomb," however this was simply an invention created to sell newspapers after the discovery of the child-pharaoh's burial chamber. Those who unearthed the chamber and remains of Tutankhamen did not die statistically sooner than others of the time-period.

Exactly how Tutankhamen died is still debated to this day. The evidence is that he had a broken leg near the time of his death which became infected. He also carried malaria. He could possibly have suffered from epilepsy. Regardless how he died, the poor kid had a lot going wrong.

The pharaoh who succeeded Tutankhamen was Ay. Ay would only rule for four years, and he would be the last of the Amarna pharaohs. It is possible that Ay was regent during the time of Tut, although this is uncertain.

With Horemheb, the eighteenth dynasty would come to a close. He would work to undo the Amarna philosophy/religion that had been instituted by his predecessors. He destroyed many monuments of the previous pharaohs, and would often reuse them for his own means. He was likely childless at his death. This brought the eighteenth dynasty to its end.

CHAPTER 14

The New Kingdom Continue and Ends

It is with the continuation and end of the new kingdom that this book will end. Although ancient Egypt would go through a third intermediate period, a brief attempt at revival and eventually come under the rule of the Greeks and later, the Romans, the fall of the new kingdom was in many ways the end of the road for the grandiose history of Ancient Egypt.

The first pharaoh of the nineteenth dynasty was Ramses I. He ruled for a very brief period, and not much is known of his reign, other than that it was a time of transition from the eighteenth dynasty to the nineteenth.

Ramses I's son, however, would undertake campaigns to attempt to restore the grandeur which was seen in the eighteenth dynasty. He would attack the Hittites and the Libyans, and would even take the great city of Kadesh, however, he would return the rule of this city to Hatti in an attempt to make peace.

Ramses II (also known as Ramses the Great and often known for his role in the story of Moses) would attempt to retake Kadesh. Ramses II had a very long rule as pharaoh (approx. 1279-1213 B.C.) During this time, he would battle against pirates, campaign in Syria many times and send armies against the Nubians and the Libyans.

During the early years of his reign, however, Ramses II was much more concerned with building. He would build monuments, temples and even cities such as Pi-Ramesses where he would establish a new capitol in Egypt. This city was located in a very meaningful place. It was built on the ruins of Avaris, the city from which the Hyksos had reigned.

Under the rule of Ramses II, Egypt had an enormous influx of wealth due to his many military campaigns and tributes paid him by the peoples which he conquered. Ramses is thought to have died at around the age of ninety having become quite unhealthy due to severe arthritis and dental problems.

One interesting fact about Ramses is that his hair was blonde, but he likely dyed it red using henna, an herb.

After the incredibly prosperous rule of Ramses II came Merneptah. The thirteenth son of Ramses II, he was the oldest surviving child of his father at the time of the old pharaoh's death. He would have been late in life himself, particularly for the time-period, aged somewhere between sixty and seventy years old. He would send military campaigns like his father, although not nearly to such a great extent. It is with the successors (note the plural) of Merneptah that things would really start taking a nose-dive in the great land.

Seti II was the rightful heir to succeed Merneptah, however, his reign was challenged by Amenmesse from Thebes. Amenmesse would take a great portion of Upper Egypt, including the kingdom of Kush. Although Seti II was able to retake the lands which Amenmesse had claimed, the infighting was becoming great within the nineteenth dynasty.

Siptah, the son of either Seti II or Amenmesse, would be the second to last ruler in the nineteenth dynasty. Like Tutankhamen, he would die at a very young age and may or may not have actually held complete control of the station of pharaoh, as his stepmother Twosret was regent due to his youth. She would rule after his death for a period of only two years or so. With her death, the nineteenth dynasty would end.

Setnakhte was the first pharaoh of the twentieth dynasty, and would only enjoy a very short reign. It's not entirely clear how he came to power, as he was of no blood relation to Siptah or Twosret. It's possible that he usurped the throne. During his short time as pharaoh, he did, however, manage to largely stabilize Egypt, although this would not last long.

The son of Setnakhte was Ramses III. Often considered to be the last pharaoh of the new kingdom with any remarkable power or control over the land, the reign of Ramses III would see near-constant battle and invasion. Due to the constant warfare, the wealth of Egypt would not-so-slowly diminish and leave a weakened nation for his son to inherit.

Ramses IV was what we would now consider middle-aged by the time he took the throne. His father had ruled for approximately thirty years. He would begin many building projects, but his reign was cut short as he died after only five or six years as pharaoh.

Ramses V's (if you're starting to notice a pattern of names, you're on the right track) reign would be marked by the growing influence of the cult of Amun, and the continued decrease of the wealth of the pharaoh and Egypt (often due to the demands of the priests themselves.)

The rules of Ramses VI, VII and VIII were similar in a few ways: First, they all ruled for short periods of time (Ramses VI for about eight years, Ramses VII for about seven years and Ramses VIII for about one year.) Also, the state of Egypt was declining faster and faster at this point. Even with the building projects of Ramses IX who enjoyed a much longer reign (about eighteen years,) the pharaohs were on a steady downward decline, and it didn't seem like there was much to be done about it.

The last two pharaohs of the twentieth dynasty (final of the new kingdom) were Ramses X and Ramses XI respectively. It is my opinion, although unconfirmed that these rulers had stuck with the name Ramses so long as an attempt to recapture the glory of Ramses the Great (Ramses II.)

Not much is known of Ramses X's short rule, and the exact period of his reign is still largely disputed for this fact. With Ramses XI, however, an increase in longevity would not postpone the fall of the once-great new kingdom of Egypt. Ramses XI would rule for a length of 29-33 years.

Civil unrest, increasing times of drought and famine and the loss of Egypt's wealth would lead to the end of the twentieth dynasty and the new kingdom. This would lead to the third intermediate period.

CONCLUSION

The end of the new kingdom marks, in many ways, the end of Egypt as it once had been. The great pharaohs and times of prosperity had passed and Egypt would slip into a third intermediate period, including subjugation by the Persian Empire.

Though the new pharaohs would temporarily throw off the fetters of their Persian overlords, the late period, as it was called, would be short and control of Egypt would eventually fall back to the Persians.

Egypt, once grand and autonomous, would see many other conquerors after this time, including Alexander the Great (who was named pharaoh without a fight, due to his decimation of the Persian forces and, well, basically everyone else he ran across.) The Greeks would continue to rule Egypt, being followed by Romans and Byzantines.

I hope that you have enjoyed this journey through ancient Egypt and its history. We've come through unification to great pyramids, from collapse to rebirth (a couple of times,) and finally to the new kingdom and the great pharaohs of the eighteenth and nineteenth dynasties.

The history of Egypt is long and complicated. There is much that is left unknown, dates are almost always disputed and there's no way of knowing (at least at this time) how many pharaohs and great achievements are missing from the histories. That makes what we do know about Egypt all the more special.

Ancient Egypt lasted longer than most civilizations have even existed, and modern Egypt lives today. Though many things changed during, and many more have changed since, the old, middle and new kingdoms, ancient Egypt still fascinates and inspires us with one of the most intricate and complicated histories of any civilization that has ever existed.

Though there is much that we still don't know about this powerful, often enigmatic place and time, new expeditions are still going to try to uncover the breath of the past. As technology grows more powerful, it's likely that what we know of ancient Egypt will continue to grow throughout the coming years, decades and centuries.

I hope that you have enjoyed this look at ancient Egypt as much as I have enjoyed studying and writing it.

The mark of history is a flame passed from one society to all others. One can only wonder what will be written about our society in the times to come.

PART **3**
ANCIENT ROME

Ancient Secrets of the Romans

INTRODUCTION

Rome. Where does one even begin? Yes, beginning at the beginning is usually the way to go, but with Rome, there were always new beginnings.

From the first king of a then inconsequential settlement to the most powerful of the Caesars, Roman history has inspired and fascinated every generation since its inception.

If you've read the other books in this series, you may notice something different at the outset: This text is much longer. While Egypt ruled for a greater amount of time than Rome, its records aren't as extant as that of the latter. While Greece would go to inspire and even become a portion of the Roman way of life, it was Rome that conquered. Put simply, there are so many sources, from Gaius Suetonius Tranquillus, most famous for his "Lives of the Twelve Caesars," to the senator and historian Tacitus, from Titus Livius Patavinus's "Ab Urbe Condita Libri" ("Books Since the City's Founding,") to Lucius Cassius Dio who wrote his histories in Greek, that it's clear: the Romans knew that theirs was a special culture.

That's not to say that Rome was without its troubles. There were constant wars, even among the Romans themselves. Slavery was common and Rome saw its share of megalomaniacal rulers. Through civil unrest and invasion, Rome's landscape would change frequently throughout its existence.

This book focuses on the period beginning with the founding of Rome to the fall of the Western Empire. Care has been taken to include as much relevant history as possible within the space of this book, but with Rome, there is always more to know. With so many events shaping Rome, its people and its influence, it's difficult not to want to include everything ever written about this great civilization, however impractical it may be. What this text has become is much larger than how it begun and I hope you find within these pages knowledge and intrigue, love, wisdom and capricious folly. There was certainly more than enough of these in Rome.

CHAPTER 15

From Village to Empire: The Humble Beginnings

While the Romans were one of the best at record-keeping among the ancient civilizations, exactly how Rome came to be was lost to antiquity, even during the time of the Empire. What we do know is that Rome was once just one of many settlements in modern-day Italy and, believe it or not, it began as a rather humble one at that.

Long before Rome was even conceived, the peoples of the area had begun settling along the banks of the Tiber River. As you'll find in even modern developing towns and cities, the single most important factor in any settlement is the availability of water. With water comes plants and animals, everything a fledgling settlement will need to survive.

Rome itself was founded during the Iron Age, much later than the Egyptian civilization and around the time that Greece began its ascent toward its own empire. The history of Rome begins, so the records tell us, on April 21, 753 BCE. Now, this is very, very specific. Does this mean that Rome, the settlement, was founded on this date, or was this the beginning of the empire itself?

The truth is that the date April 21, 753 was actually applied many centuries later by a Roman scholar named Marcus Terentius Varro. This date, while almost certainly inaccurate, does come as a result of something rather fundamental to Rome and its citizenry, though: Its mythology.

Exactly how and when Rome was settled is unknown. What we do know is what the Romans believed. Now, generally, I like to keep history and mythology separated for the most part, but in a case such as this, where the two go hand-in-hand, I think it's sapient to break from the norm and go with both, starting with the mythology.

The mythic origins of Rome are actually highly reliant on the mythology of another up-and-coming superpower, the Greeks, and has similarities to a tale from yet another tradition, that of Moses.

Rome, or so the Romans believed, was founded by two brothers, Romulus (for whom Rome got its name) and Remus. Before we get into Romulus and Remus, though, there's a bit of background information that is necessary to set the scene. The tale, which can be found in a number of ancient sources, is generally as follows:

During the Trojan War in Homer's epic poem, the Iliad it was prophesied that not only would Troy fall, but that nearly all of its inhabitants would be lost in the struggle, either to death or to slavery or to another horrible fate. This was true for all except for Aeneas. Now, Aeneas was the son of two important figures, a Trojan leader called Anchises and the Greek goddess of love and beauty herself, Aphrodite, although, in the Roman history/mythology, her equivalent, Venus, is generally transposed as the mother.

The battle of Troy is covered in another book in this series, Discovering Ancient Greece, but what is necessary to know here is that, while many fell or were captured during the sacking of Troy by the Greeks, specifically the Spartans. The Spartans were known throughout the ancient world, both in mythology and in historical fact, as extremely accomplished warriors. When Greece herself was under attack, it was often the Spartans who were first called upon, as they were better trained militarily, and were capable of winning battles that other groups simply couldn't. So, when Troy was infiltrated by the Spartans, it's fairly elementary to deduce that the Trojan people were in a great deal of trouble.

Aeneas, however, was fortunate enough to escape his burning city and he began his search for fortune and fame. His many adventures eventually led him to Italy, where he was greeted, as heroes often are, by the local king. The king's name was Latinus; sound familiar? Latinus was so impressed by Aeneas that he gave the young warrior one of his daughters to marry. The daughter's name was Lavinia.

Aeneas held his new wife in such high regard that, when he created a new settlement in the Italian countryside, he named it after her, calling the village Lavinium. Now, Lavinium grew very quickly and soon found itself as the head of a group of cities called "The Latin League." (More on that later.)

Aeneas then had a son name Ascanius. Ascanius would take over when his father died. He, Ascanius, would go on to settle a village called Alba Longa. Ascanius and Alba Longa would set the stage for the birth of Rome. Another moniker for Ascanius, during the time of the Romans was Iulus. Given that, as fans of Indiana Jones and the Last Crusade will already know, in the Latin alphabet, the letter "I" makes a "J" or "Ya" sound. Iulus was later claimed by one of, if not the most famous of the ancient Romans, Julius Caesar, to be one of the latter's direct ancestors, thus making the first Caesar also a direct descendant of the gods. This type of claim is not unusual, especially in the ancient world. The Egyptian pharaohs, for instance, all claimed to be descended from their god Horus. We'll look more into the Caesars later, though.

Now, Ascanius would be followed by twelve rulers, or kings, and it's with the twelfth king, Numitor, that things start to get really interesting.

Numitor is of vital importance to this tale for a couple of reasons: First, he was usurped by his brother, Amulius, who killed Numitor's son in the process, and second, because he had a daughter named Rhea. Amulius, like most rulers of mythology and throughout history, was fearful that he would be the target of retribution, due to how he had overthrown his own brother. Therefore, in order to ensure that neither Rhea Silvia, nor her descendants would ever be a threat to his seat of power, Amulius installed Rhea as what was known as a Vestal Virgin.

Vestal Virgins were devotees of Vesta, the virgin goddess of the "hearth fire," a symbol of permanence to those who would become Romans. The virgin part is rather self-explanatory, and very strictly enforced. In fact, if a Vestal Virgin were to become pregnant, even if the conception was through rape, the "offender," that is: the Virgin, would be punished by being buried alive.

The Vestal Virgins did not take lifelong oaths to their order, but were in this service for a span of thirty years. The first decade was spent being taught the proper rites and practices by the previous generation of Virgins, the second decade was spent in the actual performance of these rites and the third was spent teaching the next generation of Vestal Virgins so that they, too, could perform the proper rituals of Vesta.

Now, despite her new position, as with many other legends, things were about to be set right through intervention by a god.

Mars[1], the god of war and of vengeance, took a particular liking to this new devotee of Vesta and impregnated Rhea. This particular process is a rather familiar one throughout many different systems of belief. Zeus would come to the then childless Danaë, who would then bear the hero Perseus, the warrior who defeated the gorgon Medusa (see Discovering Ancient Greece.) The Christian God would do the same with the virgin Mary, though in the form of a dove, rather than that of a golden rain as Zeus had done with Danaë, and so on.

Though a Vestal Virgin, Rhea was now pregnant with twins. They would be named Romulus and Remus. Now we're getting somewhere.

Amulius was filled with rage when he found out that Rhea, daughter of Numitor, had become pregnant. He so ordered Rhea to be imprisoned and the two children killed. He sent a servant to do the terrible deed

---

[1] In another telling, it wasn't the god Mars, but an unknown assailant who fathered Romulus and Remus by raping Rhea Silvia. In this version, Rhea would simply replace her rapist with the god Mars, as she would be less likely to be ostracized for this, especially as one who served Vesta as one of the latter's Virgins.

to the newborn twins, but the servant, upon finding the children took pity on them and, rather than killing them, the servant would set the two babies adrift on the Tiber River. The river, overflowing at the time, would lead the twins to a small pool where they were discovered by a she-wolf, Lupa, who had, ironically fortuitously enough, just lost her own cubs. This wolf would act as the new mother of the twins, allowing them to suckle from her, thus ensuring their survival.

The twins were eventually found by a shepherd named Faustulus. They would then be raised by this new man and his wife, Acca Larentia. Things also took a turn for the better for Rhea, who was rescued and betrothed to the god of the Tiber River, Tiberinus.

Romulus and Remus would grow up to be strong and fearless warriors. One of their first acts upon coming of age was to return to Alba Longa and slay Amulius, and thus returning their grandfather, Numitor, to the throne.

Then, on April 21, 753 BCE, Romulus and Remus would construct a large wall. This was placed around a settlement. The settlement would get its name from the former of the two brothers. It was (and, incidentally, still is) called Rome.

This, according to the mythology of the Romans themselves, is how Rome came to be. While the twins were of ultimate importance to the founding of Rome, their triumphs would be short-lived. Romulus killed his brother Remus when the latter, in a show of hubris, no doubt, jumped over the walls of Rome. This made Remus so angry that for the massive leap, Remus was killed. Romulus, during his rule of Rome itself (more on that in the next chapter,) on the other hand, would be lost when, down at the Tiber riving, performing his sacrifices, a mighty storm arose. Many of the people fled, but the early senators stayed with him. What was believed by the Romans was that this was the point where Romulus was lost forever, but even they only had theories as to how this happened. The two most popular theories among the Romans were that Romulus was either exalted and taken up to join the gods, or, like Julius Caesar, who claimed to be a descendant of Romulus, he was killed by the senators themselves.

This wasn't the absolute end for Romulus, though, as he did later come back as the god Quirinus, one of the original Trinity of Roman gods, and the one for whom Quirinal Hill in Rome is named.

So, there's the mythology, but what is the truth? The exact origins of the settlement which would become Rome aren't known, apart from the fact that it began as a small, out of the way town in the Italian country-side. However, as is often the case with cities and/or civilizations which become great and powerful, it made more sense to the Romans that their capitol and the base of what would become the Roman Empire, should have these much grander origins.

Rome was simply one of multitudinous settlements in the Bronze Age. As the old adage goes, Rome wasn't built in a day. In fact, it's much more likely that the history of Rome itself began much earlier through the nomadic movements of the Paleolithic and Neolithic eras, through the Bronze Age and finally meeting its culmination of growth during the Iron Age.

CHAPTER 16

The Early Days, Its Kings and Its Characteristics

Back to somewhat firmer history now, as we'll take a look at the early days of Rome and try to discover what made this once-insignificant, out-of-the-way, Podunk town, the main seat of power for centuries in the ancient world.

When one thinks of those who ruled Rome, the senate may come up, but what's more quick to the mind are the emperors. However, Rome wasn't always an empire or a republic. In Rome's early days, it was ruled by kings.

As we've already seen, Rome began as a small settlement, but it's likely that its proximity to other settlements was the catalyst for its initial expansion. In Rome, there are seven hills, Aventine, Capitoline, Viminal, Caelius, Esquiline, Palatine and Quirinal, the last four of which started to be settled by small farmers. These four hills would become the major four regions of Rome.

So, Rome began as a farming community, or rather, as a small grouping of farming communities.

Now, as so often happens in ancient cultures and more modern cultures, exactly what happens next is a mix of fact and fiction, of history and myth. It *is* known, for instance, that in the early days, Rome was controlled by Kings. These early kings, much like the gods or early myths about nascent rulers of other societies and cultures, are often credited with the discovery or implementation of various things which became common later in Rome. What isn't known, for the most part, is who these kings were in point of fact, as many of them were claimed to be various mythological beings; the first being Romulus himself.

The reign of Romulus, said to occur between 753 BCE when Rome was founded to 716 BCE according to the Romans, was most notable for the interaction between the Romans and a neighboring group called the Sabines. This is often, misleadingly referred to as "the rape of the Sabines," however, what the Romans were using was the word "rapere" which translates from Latin into "seized," and is unlikely a reference to rape as we know it today.

The capture of the Sabines occurred when, after inviting the neighboring tribe to join them, the Romans, in their festival for the god Consus, the protector of grains, or the god of grain storage. When the Sabines arrived, the women were captured by the

Romans. This, naturally, didn't sit well with the rest of the Sabines, and so they attacked Rome, taking the hill Capitoline. At this point, the Romans relented and the two groups assimilated into each other.

While this story is certainly possible, it may very well be myth, although there is much that the Romans assimilated of the Sabines into their own culture.

Romulus was also said to have created the senate, although this is highly unlikely, both as Romulus was at best a highly fictionalized person, but more likely a myth in entirety, and also due to the fact that while Rome did develop a senate and form the structure of the Republic which was to be in existence, to one degree or another, throughout most of Roman history, it's unlikely that a full senate was instituted from the very first king. It is, however, true that the kings of the Romans were generally selected through the choice of the people.

The next king, after Romulus's disappearance (or possible death,) was a Sabine prince named Numa Pompilius (715-673 BCE.) Pompilius is credited with a number of things, firstly that of bringing the Vestal Virgins, discussed in the last chapter, from their original home in Alba Longa to Rome itself.

It was in Vesta Hall that the Virgins would bring the undying flame, a symbol of the goddess's favor of the area and the permanence of Roman ideals and power.

Pompilius was also credited as the one who altered the ten month calendar into the twelve month calendar. Ostensibly, Pompilius was also credited with instituting and organizing the first cults of Rome and the priests thereof. He was also credited with the construction of the temple of the god Janus, god of beginnings and transitions (often doorways.) This temple was often the quickest way for the Roman people to get news about the most basic state of war or peace, as its doors would be open in times of war and closed in times of peace. This was symbolic of when the gates of the city would be opened to allow the Roman armies passage on their way toward battle.

The third of the early kings was named Tullus Hostilius (673-641, possibly 673-642, BCE,) a Latin ruler. Alba Longa, as you'll remember from earlier in this text, was the home of the ancestors of Rome's founders, Romulus and Remus. According to the Roman histories, it is said that Alba Longa would meet its end under the reign of Hostilius. The armies of Alba Longa would attack Rome, thus incurring its wrath. As penalty for the attack, Alba Longa was said to have been destroyed by Hostilius. While it's unclear whether this particular altercation took place, it is much more possible that Hostilius was a real person, or at least based on a real person. It was also under Hostilius, ostensibly, that the home of the senate, Curia Hostilia, was constructed.

Hostilius, unlike many of his predecessors, was not particularly concerned with ritual or religious matters for most of his reign. It wasn't until, near the close of his reign, Rome came under attack by the gods that this began to change. One of these, much like one of the biblical plagues in Egypt, was a hard shower of rocks. In penance for the misdeeds, specifically Hostilius's neglect of the Roman traditions, the people performed a nine-day ritual or festival was performed. This was called novendialis.

The fourth king of this era was Ancus Marcius (641-616 BCE,) and it would be under his rule that Rome began searching to annex territories outside its own walls. He is credited as being the first to build a bridge over the Tiber River, making travel for the Romans much easier and more efficient. He was initially installed as an interim king (interrex,) by the senate, however, he held onto the throne when the people of Rome declared him King. He, like Pompilius, was a Sabine.

During his reign, Marcius would conquer many cities, absorbing their inhabitants into Rome, either through migration of the refugees, or by installation of Roman leaders within those particular cities. Originally thought to be weak, as his initial installation as interrex was largely in order to maintain the peace and prosperity that was found under his predecessor. Those who sought to take advantage of this perceived weakness would find themselves swiftly and often completely obliterated, however. He is also credited with the first aqueduct, and the port of Ostia. Through the building of bridges, aqueducts, ports, as well as the conquering or conversion of other cities and peoples, Marcius is credited for being one of the first, if not the very first, to grow Rome's borders and regional influence.

One major thing credited to Marcius was the manner of Rome's declaration of war. In order to ensure the favor of the gods, Rome would begin by sending the enemy city a runner or messenger, whose job was explaining what the offending city had done to cause Rome injury. Also contained within the message was what Rome expected in reparation for whatever real or perceived damages had been done by the offending group. If the toll was paid, Rome would usually forego all-out war. If, however, the offending city did not follow the conditions set forth in the communiqué, the Fetiales, a special order of Roman priests, would throw a spear into the enemy territory.

The fifth king of this era was Tarquinius Priscus or Tarquin the Elder (616-579 BCE.) Tarquin the Elder, like Romulus and many of the other early kings, is likely, if not in whole, then in part, mythological. He was the first of the three Etruscan kings. Etruscans were a much older group of people, and were the very first to learn and teach the skills of reading and writing. They were also a group with whom Rome would often do battle.

Tarquinius was widely considered to be a just and honest man. He was also a friend of the king Marcius. Largely at his wife Tanaquil's urging, Tarquinius, after Marcius's death, approached the fallen ruler's sons, suggesting himself as the next in line as ruler. Due to his relationship to their father, and his rather positive reputation, the sons of Marcius agreed and Tarquinius assumed leadership of Rome.

Tarquinius was considered to be a very successful ruler, however, due to his implementation of Etruscan traditions, specifically of games and the introduction and implementation of a more suitable drainage system. As so often happens, both in myth and in reality, however, it was Tarquinius's success itself that led to his downfall.

The sons of Marcius, who had previously been so generous to the friend of their father, began to fear that, due to his success, the descendants of Tarquinius may begin a more hereditary rule than had previously existed in Rome. Therefore, to prevent the stewardship of Rome becoming one of heredity, the sons of Marcius had Tarquinius killed, bringing a swift and terrible end to the mighty king's rule.

This, however, did not exactly have its intended effect, as Tanaquil, Tarquinius's wife, had other plans.

It wasn't a direct descendant of Tarquinius who would become the next king, but husband of the fallen ruler's daughter. His name was Servius Tullius.

Servius Tullius is one of the kings of this period more generally thought to have been a real person, as his name is of plebeian[2] origin, whereas mythological kings almost always, in Roman culture at least, had patrician[3] names. In fact, the name Servius itself is very similar to the word servus, meaning slave. In some versions of this history, Servius Tullius was actually, at one time, a slave before marrying the daughter of King Tarquinius.

Despite his (likely) humble origins, Tullius would go on to be one of the most influential rulers in developing Roman society into what it would become. Among his many accomplishments were the introduction of the worship of Diana, the institution of a census and he is credited with building a portion of Rome's walls which have survived, though in ruins, throughout the millennia.

Most influentially, however, was the institution of military classes and the strengthening of patricians over their poorer counterparts, the plebeians.

---

[2] AKA commoner, or member of the lower class in Roman society.

[3] AKA a member of the nobility, or the upper, ruling class in ancient Rome.

Though the citizenry of Rome all had a vote in the various governmental actions, these votes were not counted equally. A patrician vote was considered much more important and carried a great deal more weight than that of a plebeian vote. This class distinction would carry over into the army under Tullius, as those who came from nobler families would be provided with better equipment, the richer among them were even given gold with which to purchase horses. The plebeians in the Roman military, however, were provided with only rudimentary weapons, all the way down to rocks or sticks. They made up the infantry.

This incredible gap in income and social status was the source of many episodes of infighting within Rome from its very inception, on through the height and decline of the Roman Empire.

The final of the Roman kings was Lucius Tarquinius Superbus, also known as Tarquinius the Proud[4] (535-509.) Much like his predecessor, Superbus was heavily influenced into seizing power. His wife, Tullia, daughter of then-king Servius Tullius, convinced him to depose her father and supplant himself as king.

Although Tullius was a very accomplished ruler, the ambition of his daughter and, subsequently, his son-in-law would not be satisfied. Just to be clear, while

---

[4] Latin "Superbus" = English "Proud"

the initial idea may have been Tullia's, Superbus was more than willing to go along with it.

As the story goes, Superbus convinced many of the patrician senators to be co-conspirators and accessories to the overthrow of Tullius. One day, the young usurper went to the senate with a group of armed men and sat upon the throne. Once in his seat of power, he then called forth the senators to bring Tullius before him. This, they did, finding the king within the Roman Senate walls and, after declaring that his monarch was nothing more than a glorified slave and accusing him of favoring the poor instead of the rich, which was (and arguably is still) the popular tradition, along with not having been put forth as king through decree of the people or through the will of the senate, among other such accusations.

The result of this action was that Superbus took the aged king and threw him down the senate stairs. While the old king's guardsmen fled, Servius Tullius wandered the street, injured and disoriented. He was then killed by Superbus's guards or, alternately, by his own daughter, Tullia.

While Superbus was then made king, the popularity of his predecessor and the manner in which he was deposed, made things difficult for him with the people of Rome.

During his reign, Superbus would find a great deal of resistance. Despite this, he was able to institute a few lasting achievements. Of the more important accomplishments of Superbus was the construction of the Cloaca Maxima (literally, great sewer.) Now, if the importance of such a construct isn't apparent, imagine what life would be like without sewers (or, for that matter, cesspools.) Seems a lot more important now, doesn't it? This great sewer would be left uncovered until 390 BCE, and still exists today.

The modern day use of the term "sewer" is not necessarily indicative of what Superbus put in place, however. While it was a tributary for human waste, its initial purpose was to drain the water from the valleys below the seven hills, thus allowing Rome to sprawl outward in a way it geologically couldn't before the Cloaca Maxima.

Along with a new and improved sewage system, Superbus is also credited with establishing the Temple of Capitoline Jupiter. The god Jupiter would become the chief deity of the Romans and his would be the national cult (sect of the dominant religion) of Rome until the Christians took this role under Constantine (more on that later.)

Superbus, however, was a tyrant who ruled with little pity and less mercy. It was likely for this very reason that he was the last of the Roman kings. His removal from office, as it were, was not, however, directly due to his own actions, but that of his son, Sextus.

Sextus was born into nobility, and so had less patience for things which were "not his." When he and a group of nobles decided to return to their homes from their siege of Ardea in order to make sure that their wives weren't using their temporary absence as a reason for hedonism and/or debauchery, all but one of the wives, that of his cousin Collatinus, were at a vast banquet and generally, according to them, misbehaving. The one who was missing was named Lucretia. She was found at home, spinning cloth with the servants of the house. It was at this point that Sextus decided he must have her, whether she was his cousin's wife or not.

Some time passed and Sextus approached Lucretia. He extorted her by saying that if she didn't sleep with him willingly, he would take her by force (rape) and then tell his cousin that she had been unfaithful with one of their slaves. Lucretia assented, seeing no other choice, but her guilt drove her to tell her husband Collatinus what had happened. Though he quickly forgave her, this would all prove to be too much for Lucretia and she took her own life.

When the news of what had happened came out, it infuriated the patricians. They chased after Sextus who, though attempting to flee, was eventually caught and killed. His father Superbus, then king of

Rome, was subsequently dethroned as his tyranny and the cruelty of his son had convinced them that kingship could no longer be tolerated. Thus, the reign of the eight kings of Rome came to an end.

While it is definite that at least some of these rulers were largely or entirely fictional, and possible that all of them may have been, the acts attributed to them are things which left a lasting impression on Rome throughout its history. The founding of the senate, although not from the mythical Romulus, would shape not only Roman history, but the history of the world. Versions of the Roman senate are still alive and well in some of the most powerful countries in the world today. The division of military liability included the formation of centuries, that is, groups of 100 warriors, divided into specific classes of soldiers. This would prove to be crucial to Rome as a military force. And the draining of the marshes in the valleys below the seven hills under Superbus allowed Rome to become more than just a few disparate settlements.

The early days, which were often typified by rulers of various origins (i.e. Latin, Sabine, Etruscan,) led to one of Rome's peculiarities, that of allowing the people it conquered to retain their religion and culture, so long as they swore fealty to Rome itself. While saying that the Romans were the pinnacle of tolerance would be a great misstep, this boon did allow Rome to take over many areas with much smaller chance of rebellion.

In the space between when Rome first began and the last king, the area controlled by Rome had increased some 600%. That's not to say that the Roman Empire had officially begun, as, even with this expansion, it was hardly larger or more influential than its neighbors. That said, though, the time of the kings set the groundwork for what would soon become the Rome that became one of the most vast and powerful seats of empires the world has ever seen.

CHAPTER 17

From Monarchy to Republic

When the Romans finally decided to abolish kingship, they had to replace it with something. While it's unclear exactly who came up with the idea, or even if it was an individual or a group, Rome would solve the issue of governance by instituting an informal constitution which would be the basis of the republic. The republic would rise in 509 BCE and remain in place for nearly 500 years.

There were, initially, three branches within the Republic of Rome: The senate, who represented the interests of the patricians, the legislative assemblies, which represented the plebeians and had the authority to install or reject candidates for magistrate and would ratify or dismiss laws or statutes, and the consuls, two individuals who were equal in their power, and akin in nature to the executive branch in the United States, specifically, the president, or the Prime Minister of parliamentary systems of government.

While these groups existed in one form or another throughout the history of Rome, it was during the age of the Roman republic that these groups would wield the greatest influence over politics and to the day-to-day affairs of the Roman people. For this purpose, an in-depth description of the different facets of these bodies here. There will continue to be references throughout the rest of this book, but it is during this period of Roman history in which the bodies of the republic were of the greatest influence. Although there will be certain specifics in later chapters, it seems sapient here to give you an idea of the governmental structure of the republic itself.

The Senate

The senate was in existence during the rule of the eight kings, thus, basically, since the founding of Rome itself. It would be one of the most long-lasting distinctly Roman characteristics, as it would also last all the way through the barbarian rule over Rome, although it lost much of its initial power over time.

Becoming a senator would eventually become part of a process called Cursus Honorum, or succession of honor. This succession was introduced long after the inception of the republic in Rome, however, it would go to typify the nature of a politician's life. It often began with membership in a military tribune (discussed in the section on assemblies,) but always required at least ten years within the military itself before *any* public office could be held. This succession would commonly go along the following trajectory:

Quaestores were among the lowest on the totem pole, and were generally made up by less experienced magistrates. This body was most notably in charge of disbursing public funds and collecting taxes.

The next up the pecking order were Aediles. This group, initially made up of only two people, later increased to four, was in charge of infrastructure, civic tranquility, some aspects of religion, water resources and food distribution, specifically corn. Being an Aedile was not necessary for advancement, however it was often beneficial as members of this group would often gain notoriety and public support that could be crucial to their future advancement.

Next up were the praetors. These individuals were primarily concerned with law and order. Praetorship was necessary for individuals to become governors or command military units, the latter of which, called imperium, was one of the main powers of the office. There were two specific types of praetor: those concerned with business within Rome itself, praetor urbanus, and those whose duties focused on the other territories under Rome's control, or in dealings with non-Romans. These latter praetors were called praetor peregrinus. Despite the often increased duties of the praetor peregrinus, praetor urbani, those delegated to the city, often gained more prestige due to their visibility within Rome. All praetors, however, were considered to be extremely influential and held a large degree of honor within Roman society.

Higher than even praetors were consuls. This group will be discussed in greater detail further in this chapter, but there are a few specifics that bear mentioning here. Consuls, like praetors, had imperium, but were seen as higher ranking individuals. For instance, if a praetor's imperium order conflicted with that of a consul, the praetor's order would be ignored and the consul's enacted. Another, and much more lasting perk of being a consul was that consulship granted the consul's family members, including descendants nobility. For this reason, despite there only being two consuls at any given time during the republic[5], this post was highly sought. Consuls served one-year terms, and were required to be forty-two at the time of first consulship. More on consuls later.

These were the posts which senators could take, in addition to senate member. Most of these positions served one-year terms and, generally, could be filled by the same person more than once, should one choose to do so. Although, there were some regulations that a person could not serve consecutive terms,

---

[5] This would change greatly under the reign of the emperors.

such as those regarding consuls who had to wait ten years between terms of consulship.

The senate of the republic was initially made up of 300 individual senators, though this number would fluctuate in time. While the decrees of the senate were not legally binding, they were passed out to the various magistrates of the legislative branches of the commoners, or plebeians. These decrees, called senatus consulta[6], were generally followed, though in law they were no more than advice to the legislative assemblies of the plebeians. It was through the senate and their senatus consulta that the patricians retained, and even gained power.

These consulta were largely concerned with setting precedent to guide legal action, including, but not limited to, prosecution and penalties for crimes, suggested courses for military action and general governance. One of the most powerful things a senatus consultum could do was serve to interpret a given law or statue and, for this reason, they often had more power than they may have originally been intended to employ. This, however, was checked by the supremacy of the laws passed by assembly, although this was often more used in theory than in practice.

---

[6] This is the plural form of the word, the singular being senatus consultum.

One of the key powers of the senate was that it was the only governmental body that could allow disbursal of funds from the treasury. No other body had this power. Also among the senate's formal powers was that it installed magistrates over different areas or provinces of Rome. The senate could also declare anyone an enemy of Rome. While this particular power was supposed to only be used in extreme circumstances where an individual stood to cause injury to Rome itself, although, it was often used as a tactic of intimidation and a way of keeping individuals not satisfied with the current power structure in check. Through these two powers alone, the senate already wielded a great degree of power, though it could be overridden by the assemblies.

The senate meetings would generally begin at dawn and go until nightfall, at which point, the session would end. At the beginning of every session, a sacrifice was made and auspices (omens from the gods) were sought.

Due to the nature of senate sessions, a few loopholes, some of which are still in use today, were used. The most easily recognizable was something called diem consumere (translation: spend a day,) this is known today by the name filibuster. If a senator didn't like a particular proposal, especially if he knew himself to be in the minority, he would often endeavor to continue talking as long as possible and bring up points that would be hotly debated by those who would follow him. This worked especially well as, in the senate at the time, every single member, starting with the most senior and working all the way down to the most junior member in order, was required to weigh-in before a vote could be taken. With no meeting lasting after nightfall, a long-winded senator could prevent any measure from passage. This was (and is) a bit of subversion to the micro-democracy of the senate itself; however, many popular, but destructive, measures could be stopped by a single man with a conscience. That is, though, a largely idealized conception of the process's usage, as it more likely found most of its use when someone simply wanted to obstruct a decree that he didn't like.

This wasn't the only way a bill could be killed before a vote, though, as it could be vetoed[7] by senate members, often a tribune. A veto would simply kill a vote, and could not be overruled by the senate. Vetoes could also be levied by consuls, officers who were also responsible for installing senators. This job would later be performed by censors, but we'll discuss both of those groups later in this chapter.

Senators were initially exclusively made up of patricians, and their terms lasted for the duration of their lives. What made a patrician eligible for membership in the senate would change over the centuries. Initially, senate membership required an individual to be a

---

[7] Trans. "I forbid."

land owner of the upper class and have served a term as magistrate. During the time of Augustus, a provision was added that, in order to be qualified as a senator, a person must have at least 400,000 sesterces (Roman currency,) though this number would quickly be tripled.

Toward the end of the time of Roman Kings, the senate had begun to hold much of the power it would have during the republic, ratifying or vetoing decrees of the king. Its power would actually wane, to a certain degree, during the time of the republic, although its power would fluctuate throughout Roman history.

Assemblies

Unlike the senate, there were multiple assemblies, each of which held a certain degree of power, and each of which could generally overturn a provision passed by vote in the senate. The first assemblies were nearly powerless, serving much the way that polling does nowadays, giving the king and the senate an idea how the common people, the plebeians felt about a given issue or decree. When Rome became a republic, however, assemblies would become the major governing body of Rome. Vetoes, as defined in the previous section, actually had no legal force, however, as the plebeians had become aware of their own power, it was generally accepted that going against a veto was to invite disaster, as the plebeians greatly outnumbered the patricians. It was due to their numbers and their consciousness of their intrinsic power that the plebeians were able to exert so much control over the government of the Republic of Rome.

It was likely due to the very fact of the senate's existence as a patrician-only body that assemblies were formed and gained so much popularity and power. Though the senate would later allow plebeians to be members, it was the assemblies which would speak for the plebs in most cases.

Among the earliest assemblies was the Comitia Curiata, or Assembly of the Divisions, an assembly which had little power other than the ratification of king's decree. This assembly was composed of thirty curiae, or divisions, of the three principle tribes of the time: The Luceres, the Tities and the Ramnes. There would be ten curiae per tribe.

Following the division of the military into class-specific centuries (groups of 100,) another assembly would be formed, this one made up of those centuries. It was called Comitia Centuriata, or Assembly of the Centuries. There were six divisions among the Comitia Centuriata. These divisions basically followed the same class structures adopted by the military. At the top, there were the equestrians, those who could not only afford better gear and equipment, but who could also afford to purchase a horse. In today's class structure, these would be akin to the top 1% of income earners. The following divisions are best conveyed through equivalent to modern class structure. In descending order of wealth, there were the equestrians at the top, the upper class beneath them, the upper-middle class below that, the middle class below them, the lower-middle class beneath that and the poor, the individuals who would be sent into war with tree branches or whatever rocks they could find on their way, at the bottom. Within this assembly, each group had, theoretically, the same amount of power in this assembly, however, the equestrians and the next wealthiest group would usually vote together. This often negated the voice of the other divisions. The focus of this assembly was most commonly in electing magistrates, or the consuls which we will discuss in the next section of this chapter.

It would be the Councilium Plebis Tributum, or Council of Plebeians of the Tribes, that would become the first, and most powerful, body to specifically represent plebeian interests. This group passed plebiscita, or laws representing the interests of the plebeians, and held an increasing amount of power. Much of this power was through the election of tribunes, a power which was only possessed by the assembly, and could veto any measure passed by senate vote.

The power which the tribunes held, specifically, that of the veto, was predicated on the ability of the plebeian assembly to declare that oppression of plebs was occurring at the hands of the patricians. This, the plebeians, specifically the tribunes, had the power to stop in an instant. One of the most important and powerful of these tribunes was the Tribuni Plebis, or the Tribune of the People. This tribune could exercise its power, were a veto to be ignored or, simply, if they didn't think they were getting through to the senate, by suspending the activities of the senate, levying fines, interfering with elections and even halting military movements. For this reason, though it wasn't law that a veto must be accepted, it generally was, for fear the tribunes would utilize one of their many powers to disrupt the actions of the patricians and the senate. This was how the commoners of Rome gained their strongest voice, and became a politically relevant group within Rome.

These tribunes were seen as the most revered of the bodies in the Roman republic, and it would be this very reverence that would lead to their eventual corruption. To go against the will of the tribunes was seen, put in modern terms, to go against the direct mandate of the people, and this was an act that would not be tolerated. When republic became empire, however, tribunes, though they retained much of their authority in theory, would always side with the emperor's decisions. For this purpose, they were allowed to exist during the empire when the only true power of the Roman state was in the hands of the emperor himself.

It is important to remember, however, that while the assemblies, especially the tribunes, had the right to overrule the senate, this was seldom done. Most of the time, the assemblies would simply ratify whatever the senate suggested. For this reason, the senate was, in practice, the greatest power throughout most of the republic.

The Consuls

The consuls had more individual power than anyone else in the Roman republic. Election to the office of consul was performed by the Comitia Centuriata, and elections were held every year in order to ensure that nobody would ever have permanent, absolute power in Rome. This, of course, didn't last when the emperors came along. While there were originally only two consuls at any given time, this number would grow as Rome expanded, and the need for qualified regional governors rose. Under the emperors, some of the requirements, such as once an individual had served as consul, he would have to wait another ten years before he might be elected to that post again, or the age requirement of prospective consuls being set at forty-two, were both abolished.

Along with the powers given to the consuls discussed earlier in this chapter, they were also able to veto, not only senate measures, but assembly decisions and even each other. This last ability, that of making the directive of the other consul null and void through veto power led to one of the most interesting powers to be introduced, and one that would eventually spell the end for the republic. When there was a crisis of some sort, usually of a military nature, the risk of the two consuls simply vetoing each other carried with it the possibility that Rome would not be able to respond effectively or efficiently. To address this, the consuls were given the right to proclaim one person dictator.

Dictators, in the early days of the office in Rome, at least, were not necessarily tyrannical, the way that dictators of the past hundred years or so are and have been, rather, a dictator was a single point from which orders would be issued. That way, rather than infighting during crucial times of decision, a single person, above veto, would be declared dictator. This actually worked really well. The reason it worked so well was in one of the fundamental provisions of the early Roman dictator: No dictator was allowed to hold the office for longer than six months. After the six months were up—more often, even before that—the dictator would be peacefully removed from office. Should the crisis last longer than six months, a new dictator would simply take over at the six month mark, to be ousted himself, either when the crisis had passed, or when the six month term was up.

The Romans had learned that they never wanted to allow a single person to hold unlimited power the way that kings had. This term limit would not always be the case, however, as we'll discuss when we come to the age of the emperors.

Generally, at least before Julius Caesar, dictators were pretty rare. In the day-to-day business of Rome, the consuls were the ultimate authority in the land. They had the ability to declare war, and they were basically put in charge of the state. Although the consuls often stayed out of the way of the assemblies, even these powerful groups would have to acquiesce when the consuls were united against them. Due to the yearly election of consuls, however, they often had trouble reigning in the senate.

So, these are the three main bodies of Roman law and politics. While there were other positions, such as pontifex maximus, or high priest, who was the head of the Roman religion, it was between the three bodies of the senate, the assemblies and the consuls that would guide the republic until the rise of the Caesars, beginning with Caesar, the general who was made dictator for life, and his nephew Augustus, the first Roman emperor.

While these were the major groups that ruled Rome, there is a bit more to say about the law and governance of Rome, herself, specifically, the Twelve Tables. These were laws meant, predominantly, to prevent patricians from simply making up laws or punishments and so oppressing the plebeians.

We don't have every part of the twelve tables, but we do have some of each. These tables were constructed to put a set of laws in place, some which had already been in common practice, though unwritten, and others which were more specific to the times. At the writing of the twelve tables, Rome was still a long ways from its expansive future, however, these tables give us an idea what kind of law the Romans of the early republic lived under.

The first ten tables were put together by a selected group of ten men, all patricians in 450 BCE. The plebeians, however, being unrepresented in the original commission, and the laws set down in the original ten tables being skewed in favor of the patricians, demanded that another such commission be convened and it was with the second commission that the eleventh and twelfth tables were added. Only one individual was on both commissions. Some say that he was allowed to work with the plebeians on the eleventh and twelfth tables as he was an honest and just man, however, it's much more likely that he had simply defrauded the second election to ensure that he would be able to maintain his own interests in the additional tables.

While it was the three bodies detailed earlier in this chapter that would make up the government of

Rome, it was the institution of written laws that would signal the beginning of the Roman republic. The nature of these laws was rather harsh by many of today's standards, but they were still in practice, in one form or another, even after the fall of the Roman republic. These tables covered such things as the rights of families (read that as fathers,) which included such provisions as a son having been sold into slavery by his father three times would become free, and that women would remain under guardianship even after the age of majority. The latter of these two was echoed throughout the world, including the United States, until the twentieth century. Such provisions still exist in some cultures and countries in the world today.

Other provisions included protections from violence from a crowd[8] such as the law which stated that no man could be killed unless execution was called for by the proper authority, specifically, a court of law. Although, the previous provision wasn't all-reaching, as someone killed in the commission of theft at night was thought to have been justly killed. Also, burials were only allowed outside the city gates; no one was allowed to hold a meeting after dark; and women were not allowed to tear their own faces or wail during a funeral.

---

[8] This is most accurately read as through riot or vigilantism, not to be confused with mafia.

The above are only a small sampling of the laws set down in the twelve tables. The tables themselves covered, in order of tables:

- Court procedure and trial laws
- Further laws regarding the courts
- Laws regarding debt
- The rights of fathers over their families
- Guardianship and inheritance
- Laws of possession (not the demonic kind) and acquisition
- Laws regarding land ownership and the rites of such landowners
- Laws regarding retribution for injury caused
- Laws of the public at large
- Laws of religion, including such things as burial, anointment and ritual
- Supplementary and miscellaneous laws. This, the eleventh table, was written during the second commission and contains laws such as that barring plebeians from marrying patricians
- More supplementary laws.

One of the most controversial laws at the time was that mentioned in regard to the eleventh table. The law against plebeians marrying patricians was originally written in order that the patricians could retain their power over the plebeians. It was overturned, however, and further laws were made which furthered the rights of the plebeians.

In some ways, the Roman republic was a very harsh, draconian place to live. At the same time, however, it was among one of the freer societies of the time. At the writing of the twelve tables, it was suggested that people first go forth and familiarize themselves with the law and then go to their family and friends and discuss the new laws among each other. They were then permitted to come forward and suggest alterations. This is particularly striking as, though most plebeians were illiterate, these laws were meant to be in the common knowledge[9].

So, now that we have the fundamentals of Roman law and governance in the time of the republic, let's take a look at some of the important events which would go on to build Rome into more than just a negligible, regional force and elevate it into one of the largest and most influential empires in the history of the world.

---

[9] This isn't an all-inclusive statement, however, as the procedure of the court and its specific vernacular remained secret for the very purpose of benefitting the patricians.

CHAPTER 18

How Rome Became a World Power

Though Rome was on its way toward becoming the entity we now think of today, at the beginning of the republic, it was still just a city-state among city-states. The world's greatest power at the time was in Greece; however, it was during the republic when things really started to change.

During Rome's time as a republic, two of the most important things the civilization ever did were set in motion. The first was discussed to some degree in the previous chapter: The codification of laws. The second, and a trait that would continue through the time of the emperors was expansion.

Rome expanded drastically during the time of the republic. Having a clear command structure and a stable government, no longer simply reliant on the plans and decrees of a single ruler went a long way toward aiding this expansion. However, it was not only the battles that Rome won during the time of the republic, but one peculiarity would serve to quell possible uprisings. It was good to be a Roman.

Despite the severe nature of many Roman laws and punishments, Rome's codified laws extended the rights and actually provided a sense of law, order and justice, even for conquered peoples. Unlike most groups throughout history, being conquered by Rome didn't necessarily mean the destruction of the offending city, people and culture, although this did happen; often city-states were conquered with little to no military action having taken place. That's not to say that Rome wasn't a militaristic society that conquered through war, however, once a city-state swore fealty to Rome, its citizens became Roman citizens. Allies who joined or were absorbed by Rome, along with one-time enemies who submitted to Rome's authority were not given full Roman citizenship immediately, however. This was a graduated process, starting with limited Roman rights and privileges and, over time, working all the way to full Roman citizenship. This usually didn't happen in a single lifetime, although in cases where this could be used as a tool to avert some kind of disaster (military incursion, famon, lack of land, etc.) the process could be quick and, sometimes, though not often, instant.

In the early days of the Republic, Roman citizenship didn't imply nearly as many rights and protections as it would during later periods of Roman expansion. However, most societies of the time either didn't have written laws, or the laws they did have served only those of the upper class or simply did not provide the same rights, freedoms or clout as the laws of the Romans. This brought a sense of greater justice and prosperity to newly conquered territories... at least for free male citizens.

Things weren't perfect, though, and not every civilization, territory or city-state would so easily submit to the rule of Rome.

Now, I mentioned that Romans weren't always so generous as to simply offer citizenship, to one degree or another, to the people it conquered. In fact, before this became a more common practice toward cities/ civilizations more willing to submit to the power of Rome (also during and after,) Rome was often terribly brutal to its foes.

One example of this can be found with the Roman conflict with Veii, an Etruscan city. The Etruscans and Rome had had a great many conflicts toward one another and were generally hostile, if not in all-out war, then at least in distaste and hatred toward each other.

Among Rome's enemies at this time were the cities of Volsci and Aquei. There is a tale of a Volscian attack on Rome, led by a Roman traitor; however, this is likely fiction. What *is* true, however, was that Rome made a peace agreement with a group around 485

BCE called the Hernici, whose land lay between these two hostile cities. Due to this alliance between Rome and the Hernici, the threat of Volsci and of Aquei would eventually quiet, as they were no longer capable of forging a firm alliance against their Roman enemies. This process took a great deal of time, however, and the treaty would not be the end of military conflict between these cities and Rome.

The above is particularly important because another city at the time, Veii, would neither submit to Rome, nor simply become irrelevant as did Aquei and Volsci. Veii would go to war with Rome, but it would lose the bout. The Romans, disturbed by the fact that they had been so flagrantly defied, didn't see their own victory as the end of the conflict, however.

About twenty years after the Roman victory over Veii, the Romans would again send troops against their foes, besieging the city. Veii, however, was in a very defensible position among the mountains and, just for good measure, surrounded by a wall. Therefore, Rome wasn't able to take the city nearly as quickly as it had hoped. For an entire decade, the Romans would lay siege to Veii. This put a great deal of strain on the Roman economy and military power, the latter due to the fact that so many of Rome's troops were committed to the siege of Veii.

Only when Marcus Furius Camillus, a general, had his men dig beneath the walls of Veii, would Romans finally be able to enter the city en masse. Once the Romans were inside the city walls of Veii, a cruel order was issued: That all within the city should either be killed or enslaved. While this order would be carried out to a large degree, it was not the complete end of Veii. Romans would remain in Veii from the soldiers who had invaded the city, all the way through to the time when Veii would be absorbed into Rome. Eventually, what was left of the Veii people, and largely Romans and their descendants in the city, would become allies with Rome herself, with whom they had been at war long before these final battles.

The Sack of Rome by the Gauls

Rome hardly won all its battles and was actually invaded and conquered, though briefly, after the Battle of Allia between the Romans and the Gauls (also called the Celts, though these groups are not always synonymous.)

The Gauls were a large, often diverse and not always unified group of people that lived predominantly in modern-day (m-d) France and extended into areas of m-d Luxembourg and Belgium, reaching into portions of m-d Switzerland, Germany, the Netherlands, and even, to a smaller degree, Italy.

It was this spread into Italy that would raise tensions between the Gauls and the Romans; however, this wasn't the original conflict. It was when the Gauls threatened Clusium, an Etruscan city, that things started to spiral out of control.

Clusium, no match for the Gaul army, sent messengers, appealing to Rome for aid. Rome answered, initially, by sending diplomats in the form of three ambassadors. The Romans had already seen a great deal of warfare just before this time, and was stretched thin militarily.

It's important to note that, at this time, the legions of Rome were not generally made up of professional soldiers, but citizens conscripted into service in times of conflict. These groups were divided into the classes described in the previous chapters with the richest and best equipped making up the middle and each successive portion outward was made up by poorer, less equipped soldiers. While this was the formation set forth in the laws and customs of Rome at the time, it was not a failsafe strategy, as any army that wanted to defeat an often undermanned Roman legion had but to flank the Roman lines and take out the less equipped soldiers. By the time they would reach the more prepared and equipped group toward the center, a great deal of the Roman legion(s) would have already fallen in battle. This often led either to surrender or flat out defeat of the early Roman legions. Despite these fundamental flaws to Roman military strategy at the time, however, Rome had done pretty well for itself in battle, all things considered.

So, the ambassadors would negotiate with the Senons (the tribe of the Gauls which was threatening the Clusians,) but these negotiations failed miserably. Not only did the Roman ambassadors make little to no headway with the Senons, in their frustration, the ambassadors would draw their swords and end up killing one of the Gaul chieftains. This act was—and, incidentally, still is—considered a breach of law and custom and an act of war.

Rather than declaring war against Rome at this point, the Gauls sent their own emissaries to ask that the men who had committed the crime be handed over to them. While there were many sympathizers to the Gauls at this point, the people of Rome, in their hubris, would not only reject the proposal, but install the offending parties as consuls. This is where insult met injury for the Gauls, and it wouldn't be long before this mistake on the part of the Roman people would have dire consequences.

What happened next was a great turning point in Rome's history. The Gauls would return to do battle with the Romans in 387 (sometimes placed at or closer to 390) BCE. On their way toward Rome, though the Gauls would pass many Roman settlements and allies, they would pass each with reassurances that it was Rome itself that had caused them injury and only it would have anything to fear at their hands. Rome, never one to shrink from a fight, would send its own armies to meet the Gauls at the post of Allia. With only six legions, the Romans would attempt to halt the progress of the Gaul army.

There were a number of reasons why this battle would go so wrong for the Romans, but three would effectively render the Roman legions useless against the Gaul onslaught. Firstly, the inequity in equipment, training and tactics within each legion as detailed earlier in this section. Along with this, the Gauls bore longswords. Even the more equipped among the Roman legions were untrained in battle against this weapon, and lacked arms that could effectively combat them. The third Roman weakness in this battle with the Gauls was that, due to the long siege of Veii, legions were slim in their numbers and economic backing was stretched pretty thin at this point.

The Roman legions fell to the Gauls, who, now with the path to Rome unhindered, would march and sack the city. Although the Gauls took most of the city, a concentrated group of soldiers and politicians would hold Capitoline Hill. The makeshift stronghold would stand strong(ish) against the Gauls for seven months, until they were finally forced to surrender. The Gauls demanded the Romans pay a fine for their crimes against the Gauls. Oddly enough, it would be the mercy of the Gauls who, really, just wanted reparations for the death of their men at the hands of the ambassadors, and the humiliation they endured when they sent their own emissaries into Rome. Therefore, when the Gauls had conquered the city of Rome and received their ransom, they simply, and remarkably peacefully, left of their own accord, returning to their own lands.

This wouldn't be the last time a foreign army would attack Rome itself, or even the last time that Rome would be sacked, however, the incursion by the Gauls would serve to change much about the way Rome would be run in its near future. Plebeians, largely spared, and already in greater number than the patricians, were able to seize a greater amount of control in Rome. This led to changes: Such as the abolition of enslavement of those in debt, land holdings were limited and would be divvied up, to some extent at least, to the plebeians themselves.

Another notable change was that of the importance and nature of the military. Not wanting to fall again, knowing that the next invaders wouldn't be nearly so gracious in their victory as the Gauls, military service and even the amount of training and quality of equipment among soldiers were greatly improved and increased.

The aftershocks of this catastrophic blow delivered by the Gauls would be long-lasting even decades after its occurrence. For one, a wall was built around Rome to prevent it from being so easily attacked in the future. Another, and even more important, change was the installation of one plebeian in every pair of consuls elected. Through this ascent of plebeians into the most directly powerful office in the land (with the exception of dictator; see previous chapter,) Roman life would reach its greatest equality, likely in its history. Due to the plebeians being admitted into this highest office, they were also de facto able to be admitted to any other office within the government. This would also lead to the institution of the most powerful assemblies of the plebeians, and without this, the republic of Rome would have continued to be skewed toward the smaller percentage of rich nobles at the expense of the plebeians.

Rome was often at war with its neighbors. Though it would suffer its fair share of defeats, though none quite so complete as that suffered at the hands of the Gauls (for a while, anyway,) it also saw a great many and decisive victories during the time of the republic. For the victories of its armies, and the absorption/ assimilation of various cities and city-states throughout Italy and around the Mediterranean Sea, Rome's influence would grow to encompass this entire region by the end of the republic. These areas included much of what is now Europe, the Middle East and even parts of Africa.

CHAPTER 19

The First Punic War

The Punic Wars included some of the most important battles of Roman history. At times during both wars, the entire Roman republic was within a breath of falling to Carthage. Normally, I wouldn't dedicate such a large section (much less two full chapters) to two wars; however, so much of import, both militarily and politically, happened during this period that it would be a disservice to gloss over the Punic Wars. That being the case, take a deep breath and prepare yourself for some of the most interesting military history that Rome, and indeed, the world has ever seen.

The First Punic War (264-241 BCE)

The next major Roman conflicts, and the last detailed in this chapter, were the first two Punic Wars; these wars were fought between Rome and Carthage.

Rome and Carthage had enjoyed a decent amount of peace with one another in earlier times, largely due to trade and a number of treaties between the two groups. In fact, not long before the first Punic War would break out, Carthaginians and Romans would fight alongside each other against Pyrrhus.

Rome, by this time, was much more than simply the city of Rome itself, its influence having spread through most of Italy. Carthage, on the other hand, actually held greater expanses of land, both around itself, located on the northern tip of modern day Tunisia, and through other parts of the Mediterranean, including large portions of Spain and many Mediterranean islands, most notably, the western portion of Sicily. It's here that our conflict begins.

As mentioned above, while Rome was either in control of much of Italy, this control wasn't complete throughout the land. There was another group called the Campanians (from the city Campania,) who, among other things, offered services as mercenaries. A group of such mercenaries were retained by Agathocles, the of Syracuse on the large island of Sicily. These Campanian mercenaries were put to work, fighting Agathocles's foes in Sicily, eventually capturing the cities of western Sicily, including Sicily and Messana, far to the north, on the northeastern edge of Sicily itself.

Agathocles had made the Campanians promise that they would not interfere with the laws or rights of the people of Syracuse or of the other regions under his control. The Campanians, however, were a rather brash group and, after Agathocles's death, they decided to take whatever they wanted, specifically, the cities they had captured for the now dead ruler. In Massana, they slaughtered the people, leaving very few in their wake, although it is written that they did generally spare women from death, making them wives. Whether this was a preferable fate is debatable. These Campanians would call themselves Mamertines.

This slaughter of the people of Massana and the division of the city among the members of the mercenary group would bring condemnation from Syracuse, the main seat of power in eastern Sicily who attacked them. The mercenaries, who generally only liked fighting battles that they were absolutely certain to win, now threatened by Syracuse itself, appealed both to Carthage and to Rome for aid.

The situation for Rome was rather complicated, as another group of Campanians had taken the Roman city of Rhegium and slaughtered many of its citizens. Though the Romans would retake the city, defeating that group of Campanians, the ordeal left a bad taste in their mouth toward the group. Rather than come to the immediate aid of the Italian Campanians, calling themselves Mamertines, they would wait. This hesitation would backfire, however, as Carthage was quick to lend aid to the Mamertines.

Although the Carthaginians and the Romans had been so recently allied, Rome feared that Carthage would use its military action to gain control of the whole of Sicily. Carthage already held the territories of western Sicily and with the large island being in such proximity to Italy and, indeed, Rome itself, the Romans were not willing to grant the already expansive rule of Carthage further land.

Therefore, the Romans would side not with the Carthaginians, but with Syracuse. Rome took a Carthaginian city on the southern edge of Sicily, thus cutting off the Carthaginian troops from possible reinforcements. The Mamertines had, inadvertent, though it may have been, just started the First Punic War.

Quickly enough, the Mamertines had slipped the minds of either Rome or Carthage, as Rome saw this as an opportunity not only to secure the eastern portion of Sicily, but the rest of the island as well.

Now, while the Romans had become effective warriors on the land, they had not developed a navy. Carthage, on the other hand, was the greatest naval force in the region at the time. Despite having armies made up entirely (or, at least, almost entirely) of mercenaries, Carthage would prove to be a mighty force in the face of Rome. Seeing their own vulnerability in this area, Rome would begin to build its own fleets and, through a bit of trial and error, actually became pretty effective as a naval power. This wasn't, however, through the use of traditional naval tactics, rather the Romans would construct ramps which, during battle, they would use to board Carthaginian ships and turn the fight to where they did hold the advantage: In hand-to-hand combat. This tactic wouldn't work for long, however, and the naval superiority of Carthage would eventually decimate the majority of the Roman navy.

The First Punic War would last for over twenty years with massive losses on both sides. In one particularly spectacular defeat, the Romans sent a massive army, in the hundreds of thousands, to the northern portion of Africa, only to receive crippling losses. In their efforts to retrieve the armies, the Romans sent a massive fleet. However, it wasn't Carthage, but extreme weather and Roman naval inexperience that would do the unthinkable: destroy the entire Roman fleet.

The Romans would lose much of the rest of their ships to their own inexperience when, upon approaching Drepana, where the bulk of Carthage's fleet was. The Carthaginian ships simply left the harbor, leaving the ships to the front of the Roman fleet attempting to escape the harbor, while the rest of the fleet kept moving forward. The ships, naturally, collided, leaving only twenty-seven of the original 120 ships afloat.

At this point, Carthage was poised to win the war. Should this have happened, it's likely that Rome never would have lasted long enough for the rise of the Caesars, much less the rise of the Holy Roman Empire, to have taken place. However, it was at or around this point where Carthage made its fatal mistake: It completely decommissioned its navy.

The Romans had not given up on building an effective navy, though its next fleet would also succumb to inclement weather. The fleet to follow this one, however, would force the Carthaginians to rebuild their own navy, a feat which, impressive though it was, had to be performed too quickly and this disadvantage would spell the end for Carthage, at least as far as the First Punic War was concerned. The Roman fleet would battle the quickly thrown-together new navy of Carthage, winning a thorough and decisive victory.

After this crushing defeat came the end of the First Punic War. Carthage, along with having to pay a fine to Rome for going to war (Rome did this quite a bit to its conquered foes,) Rome would gain control of the whole of Sicily.

The Interim and Hamilcar Barca (241-218 BCE)

During the first Punic War, though Carthage would lose, there was one general who never lost a battle.

His name was Hamilcar Barca, and he would serve as the bridge between the First and Second Punic Wars.

Hamilcar had been extremely successful, but he was a member of the losing party in the First Punic War, and so was recalled to Carthage. He and his men had won many decisive battles against the Romans in Sicily but, despite having never lost a battle and having a nearly intact army, when Carthage surrendered, he had to return and give up his campaigns. This would be one of the motivating factors that led toward his hatred of Rome and his willingness to later ignore the wishes of Carthage itself.

When Hamilcar's army returned to Carthage, things got even tense when the government of Carthage, financially overextended due to the expense of the war itself and the penalty that they would now have to pay Rome, was unable to pay Hamilcar's mercenaries. Once these mercenaries began taking their frustration out on Carthage itself, attacking it in a violent rage, Hamilcar was sent to stop the men of his former army. This, he did, although this would only be one more thing he would hold against Carthage.

As he was a powerful general and an influential man, the higher-ups in Carthage sought his advice as to what their next step should be. They were unable to pay their former mercenary armies, their countryside had, in many places, been ravaged, trade, which had been everything to Carthage, had declined dramatically, many of their people were killed and much of their previous lands had slipped out of their control. Hamilcar would make a suggestion that the Carthaginians would like, however, he had no intention of following through with it the way he said that he would.

His suggestion was that he be provided with another army, this one to be paid in advance, just to ensure that morale wouldn't start low and only get worse. Hamilcar said that he would take this army to secure the lands of Carthage throughout the northern area of Africa, and thereby strengthen Carthage and improve its resources once more. This plan was approved and Carthage would again provide Hamilcar with an army which, as promised, he paid in advance.

Although he and his army would wage a few battles through the north of Africa, his main goal with the army was to cross the Mediterranean into Spain in order to reclaim the lands that Carthage had lost during or shortly after the First Punic War. Hamilcar, though with a new army of mercenaries, was a brilliant general and he would have many victories in this expedition.

Not all of the former Carthaginian areas of Spain were so easy to reconquer, however, as it took four years of constant, fierce battle for Hamilcar to regain the territories in eastern Spain. He would, however, eventually retake these territories.

Now, Hamilcar had three sons. These sons were Hannibal, Hasdrubal and Mago. All of his sons would follow in their father's footsteps, each to become brilliant and mighty warriors. Of these sons, however Hannibal would become the most famous (more on him shortly.) As Hamilcar had been forced to return to Carthage after it fell to the Romans, though he had not lost a single battle, he made his sons[10] take an oath that they would never suffer friendship of the Romans.

Back to Spain, where Hamilcar had won many victories and reclaimed many of the Carthaginian lands. He created a settlement, naming it after himself, calling it Barcino—today, we call it Barcelona.

The Romans, being well aware of exactly who Hamilcar was, became nervous as he had enjoyed such great, though often hard-won, success in this new venture in Spain. Not wanting to simply jump back into war with Hamilcar or Carthage itself, Rome sent a messenger to discover Hamilcar's purpose. When asked, Hamilcar's response was priceless. He told the Roman emissary that he was conquering the territories of Spain in order that Carthage might repay its

---

[10] In some versions, it's only Hannibal who would take this oath, however, it's likely that all three would take it.

debt to Rome. This was certainly believable as, once Hamilcar began conquering the silver-rich country-side of Spain, he sent a great deal of this silver back to Carthage. Satisfied enough with the answer, and dealing with other problems at the time, the Romans returned home.

Hamilcar would not survive his Spanish expedition. There are numerous and contradictory explanations for Hamilcar's death, many, possibly all, of which were created to elevate his legend. It is, however, generally accepted that Hamilcar died in battle. During his expedition into Spain, Hamilcar recaptured much of the territory previously held by Carthage and established a number of new settlements, including Barcelona, mentioned earlier in this section, as well as Cartagena (originally Nova Carthago, or New Carthage,) another important city, even today.

Along with Hamilcar's three sons, he also had three daughters. While not much of note is known about the daughters themselves (even, like his sons, their exact number,) what is important here is that his second daughter was married to a man named Hasdrubal the Fair[11]. After Hamilcar's death, it would be Hasdrubal the Fair who would continue the campaign of his father-in-law and continue the Carthaginian push throughout the land of Hispania[12].

---

[11] Not to be confused with Hamilcar's son of direct descent, Hasdrubal.

[12] Spain.

Unlike Hamilcar's three sons, or at least Hannibal, Hasdrubal the Fair did not take any oath against Rome. During his relatively just and enlightened rule of the army, Hasdrubal the Fair would sign a treaty with Rome, agreeing that Carthaginian forces would not exert themselves beyond the border of the Erbo River. This directive would be followed for a while. That is, it would be followed until the death of Hasdrubal the Fair, when Hannibal, son of Hamilcar, would take control of the armies of his father.

Let's take a quick step back and see what Rome was doing during this time.

At this point in history, $\approx$241-218 BCE, Rome controlled all but the northernmost parts of Italy, where their old foes, the Gauls, were settled. There were a number of small skirmishes between these two groups, but eventually, Rome realized that if it didn't put down the Gaul threat, they might again find themselves in the middle of a war with a people that had actually sacked Rome in the past. To this end, Rome sent legions to harass the Gauls in northern Italy.

The Gauls, with about the same thought-process, only in reverse, sent the bulk of its army toward Rome itself, confident that, because they did it before, they would again be able to take Rome. This time, however, the plan wasn't to simply leave after receiving payment and surrender of the Romans.

Here, the Gauls made a huge mistake. They hadn't taken into account the fact that Rome had grown in size, strength, influence and, most notably here, military power, training and equipment. The advancing troops of the Gauls were summarily defeated, the Romans not too much worse for the wear. However, this would not be the last conflict between the Gauls and the Romans. The Gauls will have another part to play, which we'll cover in the next section.

Rome was also doing battle with pirates (yes, pirates) around this time, and so were still a bit distracted. This will be put into context within the timeline leading up to the Second Punic War momentarily.

Now, as stated earlier in this section, Hasdrubal the Fair had died. Though he was generally considered a good and fair ruler (perhaps that's where he got the title, hmm…) he would be killed by assassination. It's generally said that the assassin was a slave whose master was killed by the Carthaginians, thus exacting his revenge over the death of his master. The death of Hasdrubal would signal a shift that would bring Rome and Carthage, now under the command of Hannibal, son of Hamilcar, into war with one another for a second time.

Hannibal, now in control of the Army, would continue the military campaigns through Hispania. Things
would come to a crucial point, however, when Hannibal set his sights on the city of Saguntum. There is
dispute as to whether Saguntum was merely an ally
of Rome, or whether it was located across the agreed-
upon northern limits of the Carthaginian forces, set
by the Romans. The reason for this is that it's unclear
exactly what river Ebro was actually referring to.
What we do know, however, was that Rome considered Saguntum under Roman protection. Although
Hannibal's attack on the city would stir up great animosity in Rome toward Hannibal and his Carthaginian army, they were busy, first with the Gauls and
then with the pirates (I'm really not joking) who
hailed from Illyria, a kingdom within the Balkan
Peninsula.

Because of Rome's hesitation in sending aid to Saguntum, despite its agreement to protect the city, specifically against the Carthaginians (oops,) Hannibal
would lay siege to the city for a period of eight
months. At the end of these eight months, the city fell
completely and those who were not killed were immediately sold into slavery. This was 219 BCE.

By 218 BCE, however, Rome had defeated the onslaught of the Illyrian pirates. Because of this, they
were able to return their focus where, had they
known what was to happen a priori, it should have
been: On Carthage.

The Romans first tried a bit of heavy-handed diplomacy (their favorite kind.) An ambassador was sent to Carthage, demanding that the Carthaginians hand over Hannibal to Rome so that he could be prosecuted (I'm confident that can be read as tortured, then killed) for his crimes against Rome and its ally, or face another war against Rome. Being a haughty bunch, the Carthaginians refused. The ambassador tried to remind them what failure to surrender Hannibal would mean, saying that he offered them both the possibility of peace and the possibility of war. To this, the head of the Carthaginian senate, whom the ambassador was addressing responded that the ambassador himself would choose what he will. Carthage wasn't going to give up Hannibal, and so it fell to the Romans to decide whether they really wanted another long and devastating conflict. The ambassador said that they would have war. And so, the Second Punic War began.

CHAPTER 20

Hannibal and the Second Punic War

The Second Punic War (218-202 BCE)

While Carthage had surrendered to end the First Punic War, the defeat had caused a great deal of humiliation for them. Had it simply not decommissioned its navy, it's entirely possible that it would have conquered Rome, this book would be called "Discovering Ancient Carthage," and most of the western world would be speaking a different set of languages than the Latin-based languages that we have today. Due to this massive and confusing mistake, however, Rome decisively won the First Punic War.

However, as often happens, a conquered people who are also humiliated tend to rise against their past foes once more. It was in this way that Carthage would again seek to supplant Rome, this time through much more dramatic means. And Rome had also made a critical mistake by focusing their attentions on the Illyrian pirates and not sending aid to the city of Saguntum. Had they done this, they very well may have avoided the Second Punic War altogether.

So, both sides had made some pretty bad mistakes, but war was now upon them once more.

Now, remember all that nifty information regarding the different parts of Roman government? You're about to be glad that you read that. (For a refresher, reference the section on consuls.)

Rome was swift to dispatch its military on two fronts, each led by a consul general. One army, led by the consul Scipio, was sent to attack the Carthaginian territories in Spain, passing through Gaul (France) on their way. The other army, led by the consul Sempronius Longus, was sent to Sicily so that it could better attack Carthage itself. A third force, made up of mostly newer soldiers and the remnants of previously fallen legions, would stay put in the northern part of Italy, which Rome now controlled, to dissuade the Gauls taking advantage of the situation. Assuming everything went to plan, the Romans expected a relatively swift victory over Carthage, bringing the war to a close. Naturally, things did not go to plan.

It was assumed that Hannibal would either remain in Hispania, or attempt to return to Carthage itself over the Mediterranean Sea, which the Romans now controlled or be intercepted by Scipio's army trying to cross Gaul on its way toward Italy, and thus: Rome. Hannibal, however, had a different idea altogether.

Well aware of Rome's options, Hannibal decided not to engage either main army directly, or risk his men trying to save Carthage. He opted for option D: Crossing the Alps with his army, bypassing the armies of Scipio and having a much less obstructed path toward Rome itself. This plan was especially daring as winter was quickly approaching, not that the Alps would have been easy to cross any other time with a full army, its stock animals that carried food and other supplies and, if this wasn't already dramatic enough, elephants.

Despite his bold plan, scouts from Scipio's army would come across Carthaginian scouts. There was a minor battle between these very small subsects, but most importantly, Scipio was now aware of what Hannibal was planning. He would return to Rome as quickly as possible to warn it of Hannibal's plans, and to take control of the lackluster army stationed in northern Italy. He would send the army he left Rome with forward to Spain, where the forces of Carthage had established themselves once more, leaving Hannibal and his main army to their task of crossing the Alps.

Hannibal would lose a vast number of his troops before (by releasing those less trained among his men to return to defend Spain,) during (through frigid temperatures, sheer drop-offs, conflicts with tribes along the foothills of the alps, exhaustion, etc. ad nauseam) and after (which we'll cover shortly) the grand march through the Alps. The exact amount of troops, animals and supplies lost during this trek is unknown and estimates vary wildly, but we do know that he lost more than half of the force that began the journey by the time his army reached the other side of the mountain range. Fortunately for his men and animals, once the journey through the Alps had been completed, he allowed most of his men to take some time to recover from the bitter journey. They had reached Italy.

Those who saw less rest were his scouts. Hannibal sent his scouts forward to meet with the Gauls, hoping to convince a large number of them to join his army and thus replenishing his numbers. The Gauls, most of whom were eager to take any shot at Rome that they could, started joining the Carthaginians in droves. Another reason for Hannibal's interest in placating the Gauls was to ensure that his army would not fall under their attack. To this end, he and his men assured any non-Romans that they encountered that the latter had nothing to fear from Hannibal or his Carthaginian army, that it was Rome and Rome only in whom Hannibal was interested in attacking. This, they had done all along their way, both through Gaul and on the other side of the Alps.

This entire episode flummoxed the Romans. Nobody had imagined that Hannibal's army would move swiftly through Gaul, as the Romans were used to Gaul attacks. When Hannibal placated the Gauls by informing them of his intention to attack only the territories of Rome, and was thus nearly always simply granted passage, nobody imagined that he would take his army through the Alps. When it became apparent that this was exactly his plan, nobody thought that the feat could actually be accomplished. When it was, despite the heavy losses, the Romans stopped imagining that Hannibal would be stopped without major force.

Scipio had rallied what forces he could from the largely inexperienced men stationed in northern Italy, and marched toward Hannibal. The two armies would meet but, despite Scipio's military prowess, his men were simply not as well trained as the forces of Hannibal. Scipio would not only see his, admittedly meager, forces defeated in battle, but would also be wounded himself. Fortunately, his son, Publius Cornelius Scipio, later known simply as Scipio Africanus, would rescue his father. Scipio the Younger plays an enormous role in the war.

Although they hadn't fought the best that Rome had to offer, so far as the army itself went at least, this victory heartened the Carthaginians. At this point, even Gauls loyal to Rome started to defect and join Hannibal's forces. Rome was in serious trouble.

Elsewhere, the other consul, Sempronius Longus, was recalled from Sicily so that his army might halt the progress of Hannibal. Sempronius made this journey swiftly and, upon meeting up with Scipio and the remainder of his forces, was eager to take the fight to Hannibal.

Scipio, having just experienced the military might of Hannibal firsthand, strongly advised his counterpart-in-office to hold back, prepare his troops and develop a sound strategy before attempting to assault Hannibal's forces. Scipio was injured from his earlier dealing with Hannibal and so Sempronius was loath to listen to his fellow consul. Though Scipio, through his right as consul, could veto Sempronius, during times of battle where both consuls were present, in the interest of maintaining order and having only one person issuing commands, the consuls each took charge of the military on alternating days. It wouldn't be long before Sempronius would let his eagerness consume him and move to attack Hannibal. This was also likely fueled by the fact that it was already December, and both Sempronius and Scipio's terms as consuls would end soon, two new consuls taking their place.

Hannibal, a military genius and master of strategy, planned for this eventuality. He sent his younger brother, Mago, with ≈2,000 men to lie in wait while Hannibal sent a few advance cavalry troops to taunt the Romans and retreat in hopes to draw the latter into attacking. Sempronius quickly gave the order to march, although most of his men were either just waking or had been asleep until this moment.

The two armies were on opposite sides of the river Trebbia. The weather was frigid and the Romans had been roused early. They would be forced to wade through the frigid river, largely unfed, woken early and harassed.

Meanwhile, Hannibal had ensured that his own men had a good night's sleep, were well fed and had properly warmed themselves around their campfires. At this point, Hannibal had the choice whether to attack the Roman army after only a portion of it had crossed the river, which was customary in ambush scenarios, but he elected to attempt to win greater favor among the local Gaul tribes and so waited for the entire Roman army to cross the river. While this would mean that he would be fighting a larger force, it also became an advantage. As the last of the Roman forces reached the other side of the river and took the long amount of time required to fall into proper battle formations, they also increased their exposure to the cold. This, mixed with the lack of food in their stomachs and sleep, served to exhaust the Roman troops further. The battle hadn't even begun.

When the Romans finally had formed up and Hannibal's forces started coming into view, yet another morale killer would come: The Carthaginians had elephants, a type of animal which few Romans would have even had knowledge. Imagine stepping onto a battlefield only to find that your enemy had with them enormous beasts, the likes of which you have never seen or even heard of. Though the Romans would hold out surprisingly long, Hannibal's superior strategies and psychological warfare would put the Romans at an even greater disadvantage than they would have been otherwise.

The battle raged and the Romans really hung in there for a while. That is, while they were fighting the newly acquired forces of Hannibal. These Spaniards and Gauls would quickly take a new position, however, placing Rome between the main forces of Hannibal's army: The infantry of Carthage. The tide of the battle didn't really turn as the Carthaginians were already winning, but the tide became a flood over the Roman forces. That's when Mago, Hannibal's younger brother, and his group of 1,000 infantry and 1,000 cavalry charged in from the flank. The flood had turned into a tidal wave, and it's estimated that over 25,000 Romans were killed in this battle. Hannibal had won his first great victory against the Romans.

Things started really getting bad for the Romans when they again made the mistake of assuming they knew what Hannibal was planning. The Romans sent an army of some 25,000 men under the command of Caius Flaminius to intercept Hannibal's army, thinking that he would take a main road (which would come to be named after the Roman commander... I think it's safe to assume that things aren't going to go well for the Romans here) called Via Flamina. Hannibal, as usual, had other plans.

It was in June of the year 217 BCE that the Carthaginian general would lead his troops into the mountains (not the Alps this time) and, flabbergasted, Flaminus went after him. This was a big mistake, as Hannibal, if nothing else, was a master of the first principle of warfare: Deception. As Flaminus's troops marched through the mountain pass and approached Lake Trasimene (after which this battle is named) in pursuit of Hannibal, the Carthaginian forces would flank the Romans, coming down the slopes. Flaminus couldn't have escaped if he wanted to, with the false rearguard of Hannibal's army to the front, the lake to one side, the charging Carthaginians on the other flank and the Carthaginian horsemen who brought up the rear, cutting them off from their escape route. It's estimated that at least fifty percent of the Roman troops were killed... and it was a short battle. By this time, if Hannibal wasn't already impressive enough, he was down to one eye.

In an earlier battle (in the spring of 217 BCE) where Hannibal led Roman legions into a swamp by an incredibly circuitous route, Hannibal's eyes would become infected, one of them to such a degree that he lost all sight in it. This trek through the swamplands, by the way, was yet another disaster for the Romans.

While Rome now lay open before him, Hannibal did not move to take it. He knew his force would be insufficient to conquer Rome itself, and so he simply went past it to the south. Here is where something actually went right for the Romans.

Part of Hannibal's strategy at this time was to attempt to garner the kind of support he had received from the Gauls earlier in his campaign. So, as he went through the countryside, he attempted to recruit Romans and others loyal to Rome into his army. Unlike his earlier experiences, however, these people would rarely join him and, when they did, it was in small numbers. For this reason, Hannibal was forced to simply continue decimating the Roman countryside while avoiding Rome itself. This preserved the city of Rome, but would take a large toll on its provinces. Soon enough, though, they would make a decision that would begin to turn the tide of the war.

As discussed in Chapter 3, when Rome was in its most dire straits, it would elect a single man to the office of dictator. What often baffles people today is that, throughout most of the republic, right until it was near its end, dictators would willingly give up their supreme power, handing control of the government back to the people. The man who would finally learn how to strike at Hannibal was named Quintus

Fabius Maximus Verrucosus Cunctator, although he's better known, simply, as Fabian.

Fabian's strategy was one that Rome hadn't tried and one that would prove to be incredibly unpopular. Rather than simply throwing legion after legion at Hannibal, who was always more than prepared and was, let's face it, a genius when it came to military strategy, Fabian would lead his army near Hannibal, but would never engage him. As Fabian would follow Hannibal, he would make sure that his army always had superior position, giving the Romans the advantage, should Hannibal attempt a direct attack on them. He would also capture or kill scouts and foragers when they would leave the main body of the Carthaginian army, a tactic which would serve to slowly pick away at Hannibal's numbers, but more importantly, make it very difficult for Hannibal to keep his army supplied with provisions. This unwillingness to join Hannibal's forces on the part of Roman cities and allies would not last, however, as Hannibal continued his campaign, effectively unchecked, throughout Italy.

As stated before, this was not a strategy that was well-liked among the Romans. While Fabian's army would follow nearby, Hannibal simply continued his onslaught, burning villages and killing Romans. Despite his growing unpopularity, however, Fabian wouldn't give in to the rush-in-mindlessly approach that had cost the Romans so dearly, but which they were now screaming for. Hannibal, however, being the strategic savant that he was, used Fabian's own disfavor to his advantage. He did this by beginning to burn, and otherwise destroy, everything that was Roman in his path... everything, that is, except for any property belonging to Fabian. While Fabian himself wouldn't allow this tactic, intended to make the Romans believe that he and Hannibal had some sort of secret accord, to dissuade him from his tactics, it would only raise increased opposition toward Fabian's dictatorship.

At one point, Fabian actually had Hannibal surrounded. The Carthaginian general had led his army into an area called Ager Falernus. Here, there were many paths that would lead out of the valley, however, only a couple of these would be available for Hannibal's use. Some of these paths were under Roman control and others were on the other side of a river system that would not be easily crossed. Fabian, quite probably Rome's first leader to even come close to the craftiness of Hannibal was informed of Hannibal's location and he would block off the remaining paths with his army.

Hannibal wasn't done being, well I'll just say it, flat-out extraordinary, though. Again employing the maxim that all warfare is based on deception, after nightfall, Hannibal attached torches to the horns of his oxen and drove them in the direction of one of the paths guarded by the Romans. As it was dark, the

Romans simply concluded that Hannibal was making his move. By the time they discovered that the torches were not carried by the army itself, but by its pack animals, Hannibal had already made his escape. Score one more for misdirection.

The Romans were about to do something they had never done before. The plebeian assemblies, the only power not under the direct rule of a dictator, would elevate one of their own to a new rank that would effectively equal that of Fabian. This man was Marcus Minucius Rufus, and he was Fabian's "Master of Horse," that is, he was a direct agent of the dictator himself.

Prior to his installation in this new role, Minucius would utilize an absence by Fabian, arranged by Roman priests more than likely as a tactic of direct subversion of Fabian, to take control of Fabian's army. Fabian had, in fact, left Minucius in charge when he was called back to Rome, however, he specifically instructed the latter *not* to attempt to engage Hannibal's army. Once Fabian was gone, and thinking, for some reason, that the direct-attack strategy that had cost tens of thousands of Roman lives already would magically work *this time*, Minucius promptly engaged Hannibal's army. He would actually win this battle, though the victory was not decisive. This would only go to support the theory that Fabian's tactics were useless and that Rome just hadn't done the same thing and failed enough at it yet.

Now that Minucius had basically equivalent authority to that of Fabian, being installed as a kind of co-dictator, he assumed leadership over half of Fabian's army. This, he would lead in the Roman tradition of victory by overwhelming force. I think we all know where this is going by now.

Minucius quickly took this force and mounted a direct attack against Hannibal. After nearly all of Minucius's army was dead a very, very short time later (that day,) Fabian and his army finally stepped in, flanking the Carthaginians, causing them to retreat. Minucius, now unable to deny Fabian's strategic superiority and the ineffectiveness of doing battle against Hannibal by direct assault, gave up his newly created title and returned to his place under Fabian, no longer a critic of the latter's tactics.

Minucius would not be the last idiot—excuse me—individual to try to subvert Fabian's tactics and meet Hannibal head-on. Here we come to what is quite possibly the most famous single battle in all of history: The Battle of Cannae.

Two consuls were sent to attack Hannibal, as again, Rome was attempting to subvert the tactics of Fabian. Despite raising the single largest army that Rome had put together up until this time, the two consuls argued with one another bitterly over how it should be used in the upcoming battle with Hannibal. The

Carthaginian forces had set themselves up in a vast, open area. He sought to draw the Roman forces into battle on this ground due to an utterly brilliant strategy he'd developed for the battle (which we'll get to in a moment.) One of these consuls, Lucius Aemilius Paullus, upon seeing the area, wanted to move the Roman forces into the hills, thus providing them with the superior position. The other consul, Gaius Terentius Varro, on the other hand, thought that the sheer size of the Roman army, which was supplemented by allies from both the Samnites and the Etruscans, would be enough for a Roman victory. The Romans, by now, really should have known that it was always, *always* a terrible idea to engage Hannibal on his own terms. However, on Varro's day to be in charge of the army, his hubris would lead over 80,000 troops into direct conflict with the forces of Hannibal and Carthage.

Hannibal's strategy was as follows: He arranged his armies in lines, and these lines were arranged into a "V" formation where the tip of the "V" would be at the front of the force and each pair of lines to each side would follow a little behind. Despite most generals (Rome's included) putting their strongest forces in the middle, Hannibal did this backward, putting his weakest line in the front of the battle, his strongest forces behind and farthest from the middle on each side of the formation. He would also employ his cavalries, the Spanish and the Gaul on one side, the Numidian on the other.

The battle begun and Rome, just as Hannibal had hoped broke its lines and focused its attention on the center of the Carthaginian lines. The center Carthage line fell back, but it didn't retreat. This was ensured, as Hannibal and his brother, Mago, held the rear of the center line, assuring the soldiers ahead of them that if they were all to die, so would their leaders. As the center line fell back, the flanks moved forward and the Gallic and Spanish cavalry circled around the back of the Roman forces, focusing their attention on the Roman cavalry. The Roman lines would continue to move toward the center, breaking ranks, while the Carthaginian center continued to move back, its own outer lines moving forward still and eventually flanking the Romans.

This is where it all fell apart for the Romans. They hadn't anticipated that their focal point would be the weakest of the Carthaginian troops. When the outer lines came to flank and subsequently encircle the entirety of the larger Roman Force, the Romans realized their mistake, but it was too late. Being entirely surrounded, the Roman soldiers were slaughtered. Paullus, the consul that had advised Varro not to engage Hannibal on his chosen battlefield was slain while Varro escaped on a horse, after the cavalry was told to dismount as a sign of solidarity with the other soldiers. All told, as much as 77,000 of the men from largest Roman army that had been put together up until that point were killed with nearly all of the rest, minus a few, like Varro, who escaped, being captured by Hannibal's troops.

This loss hit Rome hard, and Hannibal was appearing to the Romans to be unbeatable. At this point, there were no Roman armies between Hannibal's forces and Rome, but Hannibal didn't attack the capitol, offered the Romans terms of their surrender. Whether this was because he felt his force inadequate to take the city, or because he believed the Romans would accept his terms is unknown. What is known, though, is that Rome rejected the terms. The war would continue.

Meanwhile, Syracuse's leader Hieronymus, after having been informed of the massive victory of the Carthaginians in the Battle of Cannae, turned coat and joined forces with the Carthaginians. Carthage would send a large detachment to secure its new land in Sicily, a decision that would weaken its armies on other fronts. The Carthaginian forces now in Sicily would suffer many hardships, and when the Romans sent an army to secure Sicily once more, the forces of Carthage would face a great deal of defeat on the island.

Carthage did have one secret weapon in Sicily, however, and that was the mathematician Archimedes. Despite the superiority of the Roman forces, Archimedes developed several genius devices and strategies that would slow Roman progress, including enormous cranes that, sources claim, were capable of lifting enemy ships out of the water and then dropping them again, catapults which would fling boulders farther than any the ancient world had seen before this point and, though this final one is the least likely of the purported war machines of Archimedes, a series of mirrors which would focus and reflect the sunlight into a single point, capable of setting enemy ships aflame. Think ant under a magnifying glass. Archimedes, unfortunately, was killed when the Romans took Syracuse. Legend has it that he was working on a mathematical proof at the time, and when the Romans entered his room, he simply said, "Do not disturb my circles."

Back in Italy, Hannibal's forces continued to make some progress through the countryside, however, utilizing Fabian tactics, the Romans would simply recapture cities that fell to Hannibal after the latter left, reestablishing them as Roman. They would also capture cities who had joined forces with the Carthaginians, leaving Hannibal's army without such a source for reinforcements. At one point, Rome, a bit too full of itself, declared that Hannibal's army was no longer a primary threat to Rome. This decision allowed Hannibal and his army to remain in Italy, largely unchallenged for about four years.

In Spain, where Scipio the Elder of the Romans had sent his army ahead, Carthage wasn't faring nearly as well as it was in Hannibal's army. The Carthaginians didn't suffer near the crushing blows that the armies of Rome had in Italy, but Scipio's son, Scipio the Younger (later Scipio Africanus; we'll see why shortly,) wanting to avenge the death of his father at the hands of the Carthaginians, lobbied the senate to make him commander of the forces in Spain. This, the senate did, largely due to the fact that there was really no one else to send. Scipio the Younger won some battles and was, in his own right, a brilliant general. He engineered a strategy that would capture Carthage's capitol in Spain: Cartagena, then called Nova Carthago, or "New Carthage."

Scipio was able to take the city due to its unique geography. The main route to the city, which was otherwise surrounded by water on nearly all sides, was wide enough for Scipio's main force to comfortably assault the city. Scipio, having paid some attention to the area, sent 500 of his troops around to the north on the banks of a lagoon, not far from the walls of Cartagena. As Scipio's main group put pressure against the walls of the city, winds rose over the lagoon, draining it enough that the 500 Roman troops were able to cross to a section of the walls which were not being guarded. These 500 would gain entrance to the city and, when the gates were opened from the inside, New Carthage fell to the Romans.

Scipio had struck an incredible blow for Rome, but he was far from finished. He would win a decisive battle over Hasdrubal, causing the latter to retreat from

Spain. Hasdrubal would cross the Alps like his brother before him, the goal being to combine their two armies. Had this happened, Rome would easily have fallen to the Carthaginian forces. Hasdrubal, however, would be killed before the two armies could join together. Due to a surprise attack by two joined Roman forces, Hasdrubal's army was thrown into a conflict against the Romans with a river behind them and no way to retreat. As it's written, Hasdrubal, realizing that his army was to fall, charged headlong into the Roman forces, wanting to do as much damage to them as he could on his way down. He was killed and his army was in tatters. In a bit of psychological warfare of their own, the Romans threw Hasdrubal's newly severed head into Hannibal's camp, causing an understandable drop in the latter's morale.

After Hasdrubal had left Spain, the remaining Carthaginian forces made a final push to oust the Romans from the Iberian Peninsula. The Romans, led by Scipio, were hesitant to attack the larger Carthaginian force. The two armies would line up in formation, day after day, only to return to their tents at night. Scipio used this to his advantage.

Day after day, Scipio would line his army up with the strongest forces in the middle. After seeing this enough times, the Carthaginians would come to expect it. Here's where Scipio took a few chapters out of Hannibal's book. He lined up his forces early one morning, this time with his weakest troops in the middle and his stronger forces at the flanks. He lined up his troops very close to the Carthaginian camp and sent a small detachment to bait the enemy into deploying its troops. The forces of Carthage realized too late what was happening, and they suffered a loss comparable to what the Romans had suffered at Cannae.

Back in Carthage itself, feuding princes and civil unrest would spell the end of the Carthaginian campaign and, indeed, the second Punic War. One of the heirs apparent had actually sided politically with the Roman forces. His name was Massinissa, and the Romans were quick to gain his favor.

With Massinissa's defection, Rome now had one of the most important advantages of the Carthaginian forces: The Numidian Cavalry. The Romans took the armies of Carthage in Africa apart quickly, causing Carthage to make its final mistake: They recalled Hannibal to defend Carthage itself.

This move by Carthage was understandable, as the Romans were poised to take their capitol and had decimated the Carthaginian forces in the area; however, they really should have listened when Hannibal warned them against sending his army and the unprepared troops left in Carthage into battle with the Roman army at their doorstep. The Carthaginian senate, however, ordered that Hannibal and his men take the field of battle. Being loyal to Carthage, Hannibal did this.

The forces of Carthage fought valiantly, but the Roman forces were too great. With the Numidian cavalry now on the side of Rome, the cavalry of Carthage was routed and the Romans were able to use the Numidians to attack Hannibal's rearguard. Hannibal's army fell to the Roman forces, commanded by Scipio (it was for this victory that he gained the title Scipio Africanus,) and Hannibal fled. Carthage would surrender and so would end the Second Punic War. It was said, although this is likely myth, that Scipio Africanus, in order to prevent any crops growing in the area, had salted the earth. While multiple sources do state that Scipio plowed the land around Carthage, an ancient way of rubbing in the fact that Carthage had been utterly dominated, sources claiming that he added salt to the process came much later.

There would be a Third Punic War (149-146 BCE,) but it wouldn't   Carthage being only a memory of its former self. In this brief war, Carthage would be beset by the Roman forces once again, this time without the aid of Hannibal (who had died years earlier in 183 BCE.) The city would fall to the Romans and Carthage, the force which had brought the Roman Empire within a breath of destruction, would itself be scattered to the winds, its city all but leveled, its people slain or fleeing for other lands. So the Romans would win against an enemy that, at times, appeared to be unbeatable. While there would be another hundred years before the dictatorship of Julius Caesar, the Roman republic had suffered greatly during the Punic Wars. It had rebuilt and the generations passed, but infighting would soon lead to the fall of the republic itself.

CHAPTER 21

The Fall of the Republic and the Rise of the Caesars

After the end of the last Punic War, things weren't all well and good in Rome. A number of issues had faced the republic for a long time, and they were only getting worse.

For one thing, those who took the role of dictator, who were supposed to abdicate after six months in office, began to stretch their terms out little by little. Each dictator would eventually give up his power, one way or another, but the underlying problem was clear: Too many people wanted too much power.

The tribunes, originally put in place for the sole purpose of protecting the interests of the plebeians began acting in the best interest of its strongest members. Consuls and dictators would conscript armies that had greater allegiance to them personally than they had for Rome itself. The Roman economy had also stalled. In the interest of saving money, Romans began using slaves more and more to do jobs that the plebeians had once performed. Think of it as an incredibly extreme version of outsourcing.

Now, the Romans had slaves throughout its history, but revolts became more common and better organized. Tensions rose as more slaves were taken and more was demanded of them. The number of slaves or freed men and women who had once been slaves is estimated to have been about 60% of the population of the city of Rome by 130 BCE.

This number had actually grown as a result of Hannibal's campaign against Italy during the Second Punic War, as the general had burned or otherwise destroyed so much of the Italian countryside including cities, villages and, most importantly in this case, farmland. Agriculture had long been (and still is) absolutely vital to the ability of any people to remain in the same place for an extended period of time. With so much work to do in restoring farmland, replanting crops and tending to those crops, much of the agrarian work done between the Second Punic War and the end of the republic had been performed by slaves.

While this seemed like a good idea to the Romans at the time, so much money was going into the purchase and maintenance of slaves (food, water, shelter, tools, clothing, etc.) that the Roman economy simply stopped growing. The only ones to really hold and grow their wealth were those who were already wealthy. It had been suggested at one point that the large tracts of land that had been distributed (primarily among the patricians) after the Second Punic War be divided up with more equity toward the poor. The previous landowners would be compensated for the land that was given up, but the wealthy patricians of the senate refused to fund an investigation into how this might be achieved, basically pocket-vetoing the whole idea.

Partially as a result of this, and partially because Rome was simply a military society that had become the dominant force of the Mediterranean of the time, Rome often went to battle far and wide, using the money and other valuables of conquered cities and peoples to bolster the Roman treasury. Expedition after expedition went out, and in a remarkably short amount of time, Rome came to expect more and more loot with every return of an army.

While this did bolster the economy for a while, it also created a wealth gap, as more money would generally be distributed to the patricians than the plebeians. Domestic tensions continued to grow out of control. Julius Caesar hadn't yet arrived to allow the gladiatorial games[13] to be free and open to all, so the people had little vicarious catharsis through which to release their frustration.

---

[13] Brutal sporting events, held in stadiums or locales of similar build.

Here, it's helpful to discuss gladiators, their schools and the arenas. Gladiators were often, though not always slaves. Sometimes they were condemned criminals, other times, members of conquered or reviled people—sometimes, they were individuals just looking to make a name for themselves. As gladiatorial arenas grew in popularity, however, the percentage of them who were slaves rose from its already high percentage.

Gladiatorial "schools" were both training areas and living quarters. These schools were often entirely made up of slaves, who would be sent into the arena, time after time, until they were killed. Just like any area where an enslaved or otherwise oppressed group was being guarded by a lesser amount of sentries, though, these schools were ripe for insurrection.

One gladiatorial slave, a man who had, depending on which source you look at, either been a former Roman soldier or a captive of the Roman soldiers, was named Spartacus. Now, Spartacus wasn't just good in the arena, he was brilliant. For this reason, he was elevated to the gladiatorial station of murmillo. Murmillos were allowed large shields and gladii—straight swords with a broad blade—both of which, Spartacus became a master of.

He and about seventy other slaves in the gladiatorial school conspired to escape. They couldn't waste much time, as it was never certain how many of them would still be alive on any given day. So they struck.

Armed with kitchen utensils and whatever they could find, the slaves revolted, killing the guards on their way out and making it free of the school. Once on their own, they recruited other slaves to join their revolt and began attacking smaller villages and settlements to gain money to better supply themselves.

In the beginning, the Romans didn't take the rebellion all that seriously. They obviously wanted to put an end to it, but hey, they were already putting down a rebellion in Hispania at the time anyway, so they didn't see fit to dedicate any centuries to stopping the revolt, rather, they simply began by sending smaller groups of untrained men. This would prove to be a mistake. The year was 73 BCE, and the Third Servile War had begun.

Spartacus is certainly the most famous of the leaders of this revolt, but he wasn't the only one. Oenomaus and Crixus, two fellow escaped slaves, were also installed as leaders. Under this leadership, the group of escaped slaves would see its numbers swell and more slaves escaped or were liberated to join the cause. Eventually, the band would number approximately 125,000, and was made up, not only of soldiers, but any slave willing to contribute to the cause.

Despite being underestimated in the beginning, the continued victory of the slave army over Roman soldiers and the continued pillaging of Roman cities, finally led the senate to see the great threat that was now facing them. The Romans would send eight legions of men—somewhere in the area of 43,200-48,000, with cavalry—after Spartacus and the slave army.

Had the slave army been composed entirely of soldiers, there's a good chance that it would have won the bout, however, with so many women, children and elderly among them, the number of warriors among them was a lot less than their total number. They held their own for an admirably long time, though, winning smaller skirmishes here and there.

When reinforcements arrived to bolster the numbers of the Roman army, however, it was clear that there was to be no survival for the slaves. And so, rather than attempt to surrender and either be killed or returned to bondage, they charged the Roman legions. It was a suicide mission and they knew it. They managed to take out a fair number of Roman soldiers, but the battle was short and the slaves were killed en masse.

This was the largest revolt of slaves at the time, but it represented a much larger underlying conflict. The only people who were happy during this period were those with power—though, they were also paranoid and constantly anticipating assassination, so calling them happy may be an overstatement—and those who sought after power were increasingly trampled. Those who already had power wanted more, and often resorted to brutal tactics to gain it. Those without power wanted it.

Now, earlier I mentioned that consuls and other high-ranking military types had begun forming armies of their own, loyal to themselves more than to Rome. It would be when one such man, a dictator at the time, was ostracized with his army that tensions would come to a head and the republic would cease to exist as the Romans knew it. The man's name was Julius Caesar.

Julius Caesar

Of all the names known today and studied in the history books regarding ancient Rome, none are more well-known than Julius Caesar (July[14] 100-44 BCE.)

Caesar was an accomplished general who had led successful campaigns through Gaul. Before this, he was once elected to the office of High Priest of Jupiter, but infighting between his family and of Lucius Cornelius Sulla, more on him in a moment, he was stripped of his title, the dowry he'd received

---

[14] Named for him.

upon marrying his wife, Cornelia Cinnus, and even of the inheritance he'd received after his father's death when Caesar was 16.

Sulla was a general with an army very loyal to him. He would lead his men against Rome, more than once, looking to take what he couldn't have through political maneuvering through sheer force. This was the man with whom Caesar's family was feuding.

Caesar's unwillingness to divorce his wife was partially, but not entirely to blame for his being stripped of all he owned. Even after Sulla was confronted by some of his own supporters, the Vestal Virgins and even Caesar's mother, he backed off, but Caesar didn't trust the mad dictator, Sulla, to leave him in peace. The result of which was that he joined the army.

Caesar worked his way up through the ranks, showing himself from the start to be a brilliant and capable warrior. Sulla died in 78 BCE and Caesar could again return to Rome.

In 75 BCE, Caesar, now a general, would travel across the Aegean Sea. On his journey his ship was set upon by pirates and Caesar, easily the highest ranking official on board, was captured. That's right: Julius Caesar was once captured by pirates. Now, the pirates were looking for ransom and Caesar was their captive. Despite this, he often taunted the pirates. An avid poet, Caesar would read some of his work to the pirates. If they didn't express admiration for his words, Caesar would flat out insult them. Most famously, upon being told that the pirates were seeking twenty talents[15] of silver for Caesar's release, Caesar insisted that they raise the ransom to fifty[16]. This gives you an idea what kind of psychology was going on in Caesar's head. Finally, the ransom (of *fifty* talents) was paid and Caesar was released.

Caesar would be elected into a military tribune, and then a quaestor. This started his political career. His wife would die during his first year as quaestor (69 BCE.) He would marry the granddaughter of the now-deceased enemy of his family and continue his political track. He obtained the ranks of Pontifex Maximus (high priest,) and the next year, praetor. Both of these elections, and likely all of his other ones, were generally won by Caesar through underhanded tactics.

Caesar would, after his year as praetor, become a governor (propraetor – someone with the powers of a praetor, but doesn't hold the office) of the southeastern portion of Spain, but before he could leave, he still had a great deal of debt to repay, thanks to the seizure of his assets by Sulla. In order to be free to

---

[15] One talent was seventy-two pounds, although there is dispute about the actual measure. This initial ransom would have been in the neighborhood of 1,450 pounds (≈658 kg) of silver.

[16] Approximately 7,635 pounds (≈1,649 kg) of silver.

leave the city, he backed his wealthy friend Crassus in challenging a man named Gnaeus Pompeius Magnus, more popularly known as Pompey. Pompey will become very important very quickly.

While in Spain, Caesar's warriors would declare him an honorary general (imperator,) a title that would make possible a great party thrown in his honor. This would be a great move for him politically, as it would bolster his popularity and public honor. This presented a problem for Caesar, however, as were he to accept a triumph, he would, by custom, have to remain outside the city of Rome until the triumph himself. What he really wanted was consulship, and for this, he would have to give up his command. He did.

Caesar won, although there were many rumors that the election was tampered with. During his consulship, he would play both sides to ensure his future gains.

You'll remember Pompey from earlier in this chapter. Caesar, not wanting to only be supported by one faction and not both, approached Pompey. He would offer the two, who had been at each other's throats for years, shared power in what was called a triumvirate (rule by three individuals.) This, they accepted, and the triumvirate would last until 53 BCE.

The triumvirate wasn't very popular with the Senate, though. The Roman bigwigs weren't comfortable with the power that the three held, and would work to dissolve the triumvirate. These efforts would soon fail, and the triumvirate would flood the senate with measures the former's members wanted to see passed, and through power and intimidation, they gained what they sought to gain.

At first everything was great between the three; Pompey even went as far as to marry Caesar's daughter, showing his commitment to the alliance. Caesar would be declared (or rather, declare himself through the senate) proconsular of Gaul. He set out with his new army, and would spend the next years conquering city after city until Gaul itself fell and became part of Rome's expanse. He would also lead not one, but two expeditions to what was considered to be the end of the earth: Britain.

Caesar was becoming the stuff of legends, and this made the other members of his triumvirate, specifically Pompey, envious. Due to a failed attempt to seduce Caesar's wife, Pompeia[17] by a rather repellent figure named Clodius Pulcher, Pompey started denouncing Caesar through implying that his wife was of an undesirable character. Every levy Pompey made against Clodius was directed toward undermining Caesar's increasing clout.

---

[17] He had a number of wives during his lifetime.

Crassus informed Caesar of what Pompey had been up to, and the three would meet in order to attempt to work out their differences (ambitions) and salvage the triumvirate. This would work, for a time, as each man was given a different territory in which to launch prestigious military campaigns. However, after the death of Crassus, the remaining two would never be on the same side willingly again.

The two men began openly opposing one another, each trying to become more powerful at the other's expense. An agreement was struck that Caesar would finish out his military campaign (at this point, in Gaul,) while Pompey would have sole control of Rome. This led to the formation of factions within the city of Rome, some for Caesar, and some for Pompey. These factions were comparable to modern-day street gangs, each vehemently opposed to the other, and they would often riot and kill one another in the streets of Rome. At one point, in 52 BCE, the civil unrest in Rome would lead to the burning of the senate house.

After the senate house was burned, the senate was quick to give imperium to Pompey in an attempt to quell the unrest. Now, the senate had been attempting to recall Caesar for some time, at first ostensibly hoping that his return would mean the end of the riots and the violence within Rome's walls (this is what led to the agreement in the previous paragraph.) The real reason for the recall, and this wasn't long kept a secret, was that Caesar had become powerful enough himself to challenge Rome. After Pompey was given imperium, he was persuaded (in 50 BCE,) although it didn't take much, to back orders that Caesar be recalled to Rome. This is where the republic would take its final breath.

Caesar returned to Rome, all right, but he didn't give up his command. His soldiers were loyal to him to a much greater extent than they were to Rome. The initial order was vetoed by Scribonius Curio, one of Caesar's many, many shills, but Pompey was being encouraged to use his own armies to put an end to Caesar. A number of compromises were offered, but the senate continually struck them down. Marc Antony, a senator and a close, personal friend of Caesar, attempted to veto a measure that would supplant the governors in Gaul loyal to Caesar with new ones loyal to the senate and to Pompey. Antony's life was threatened and he was forced to escape the city. The senate saw any scenario that included Caesar not returning to Rome on his own and handing himself over to them, as flirting with disaster. Unknowingly, these very rejections would spell the end.

The senate gave Pompey the right of Senatus Consultum Ultimum, that is, the ability to declare Caesar an enemy of the state. Caesar was already banned from reentering Italy before Pompey's imperium was up—though it's unlikely he would have been welcomed even after this time—but, defiantly, Caesar crossed the River Rubicon[18], entering northern Italy.

Caesar sent messengers to offer Pompey an arrangement where the two would share power, but Pompey refused. Caesar was now ready to do whatever it took to save himself from the senate and ensure that he would either hold ultimate power of Rome, or die trying. His forces crossed Italy while Pompey and his forces would beat a hasty retreat. Pompey's army would seek refuge in Greece. With Rome now in sight, Caesar advanced on the city. He had issued strict orders that, while the city must be taken, the soldiers were not to destroy anything, murder anyone or ransack the city. This endeared Caesar to many of the Romans, including Pompey's remaining troops (who quickly joined Caesar.)

Caesar would spend the next years chasing down Pompey and the remnants of his army. While there would be some obstacles, Caesar's forces dominated Pompey's army, though Caesar was merciful, capturing as many as he could without killing them. Pompey would retreat all the way to Egypt, where he was murdered at the order of Ptolemy the Thirteenth (Ptolemy XIII, as it were,) a child king who hoped to garner favor of Caesar.

---

[18] One of the popular stories about Caesar has him declaring, upon crossing the Rubicon, "The die is cast." It's uncertain whether he actually uttered the phrase at the time, though.

Upon Caesar's arrival in Egypt, he was shown the head of his longtime foe. Ptolemy's plan backfired, though. Caesar was furious that Pompey had come to such a fate and supplanted Ptolemy XIII in favor of his sister, by taking the crown of Egypt and giving it to her other brother, Ptolemy XIV, who she immediately married to solidify her new claim to the throne. The sister was named Cleopatra.

This action would cause civil war and thrust Caesar in the middle of it. The fighting didn't last long, however, as Ptolemy XIII would fall in battle. Caesar would leave a legacy in Egypt in the form of a son, born of the new pharaoh, Cleopatra.

Caesar returned to Rome in superhero fashion, righting wrongs along his way. He came to Pharnaces II, the king of Pontus (a province of modern-day Asia Minor.) The war between Pharnaces II and Caesar would only last five days. Caesar, triumphant, patted himself on the back, saying, "Veni, vidi, vici," or, in English, "I came, I saw, I conquered."

Caesar returned to Rome, ready to rebuild and reunite. He offered those previously loyal to Pompey clemency if they would swear fealty to him, he granted citizen or proto-citizen status to various peoples who had helped him, admitted members of former enemy tribes to the senate and cutting taxes, among other popular measures. He would seize the lands of Pompey followers and fine cities that had sheltered or otherwise given aid or support to Pompey. These last two measures brought in enough currency that Caesar was able to fund free public entertainment such as gladiatorial events, provide for his soldiers and strengthen infrastructure.

His popularity was great during this brief period; however, his need to be in complete control would be his undoing. He would be elected to the offices of consul and tribune repeatedly and be named dictator for life. He also adjusted the calendar to include his name as one of the months of thirty-one days (July.)

His haughtiness, however, led to the belief that Caesar was trying to make himself king. Although the title was different, he already was, de facto, in this position of power. Had he not flaunted it so brashly—having a throne for himself placed in the senate, including his likeness among those of gods and former kings, naming a month after himself—he might have been all right. As it stood, though, despite his popular policies which paved the way for Rome's reconstruction and growth, he had made a lot of new enemies in his quest for ultimate power.

On April 15, 44 BCE, famously, the Ides of March, Caesar arrived at the senate. He was to leave for a time only a few days later. This was the day that an estimated sixty conspirators—headed by Marcus Junius Brutus, a friend of Caesar's[19] and Gaius Cassius Longinus, an avowed enemy and critic of Caesar— had planned to assassinate the dictator. When Caesar arrived, they made their move, stabbing the dictator-for-life twenty-three times, thus ending the reign of Julius Caesar. Empire was to follow.

---

[19] Brutus's motivations were pure in comparison to those of Cassius. He agreed to take part in Caesar's death in hopes of preventing a return of the kingship.

CHAPTER 22

The Principate: The Julio/Claudian Dynasty

The Death Throes of the Republic and the First Emperor of Rome: Augustus Caesar

With Julius Caesar now dead, those in the republic's seats of power expected things to go back to the way they were. At least, that was the hope. Caesar had trampled all over the constitution, but he had been a very popular ruler. After the funeral for Julius Caesar turned into a riot, the crowd burned the forum and set out to kill the known conspirators. Brutus and Cassius, the two major players behind the assassination itself, were forced to flee the city. The people wanted another Caesar, and they would have one. The senate was beset by a populous that wanted to be ruled by lifelong dictators. The citizens assumed, rather stupidly (to put it very nicely,) that anyone to follow Caesar would also be worthy of his example. The senate had little choice but to acquiesce to the populous. The question was: Who would be the next to lead Rome?

There were two primary options, Marc Antony—who very well may have returned Rome to a republic—or Caesar's adopted son, Gaius Octavius Thurinus (better known as Octavian,) who had been adopted by Caesar and been named heir in Caesar's will. It's important here to note that the heirship to Caesar was not to his station as permanent dictator, but as heir to his estate and something akin to his political and social standing, minus the total-ruler-of-Rome bit.

Marc Antony would soothe Rome after the funeral of Caesar, allowing his killers to escape and even offering governance to Brutus and Cassius. He also kept Caesar's men away from the city, ensuring that there wouldn't be a civil war. However, Antony was very unpopular with the senate, as he had begun issuing orders, in Caesar's name, claiming they had been unsent dispatches by the fallen dictator. Along with this, he also went on a bit of a spending spree with Caesar's private treasury and the funds of the people as well. Though Antony was lobbying for the abolition of the role of dictator to prevent any one man from holding such power in Rome again, he was overruled and Caesar's adopted son was named heir.

Octavian, having been unaware of all this, was in Spain, and would receive both knowledge of Caesar's death and his own naming as heir at once. He returned to Rome, calling himself Gaius Julius Caesar Octavianus in a successful ploy to get the fallen Caesar's army to lend him its loyalty. This loyalty would probably have come his way regardless, however, as Marc Antony had spent money intended for Caesar's loyal troops.

Octavian and Antony would feud with one another bitterly, as Antony continued to use his relationship with Caesar and his newfound prominence to his own benefit. Antony would eventually leave Rome, and Octavian, in pursuit of the man who had abused Caesar's holdings and memory, set after him. The two would do battle and Octavian would win the bout, although Antony survived. Octavian, rather than pursuing Antony, attempted something to further unite the people of Rome: He offered a second triumvirate.

This triumvirate would come to pass with Antony, Octavian and Marcus Aemilus Lepidus, a close friend and supporter of Caesar's. Each would take a different territory, though all would retain some portion of influence over Rome itself.

The triumvirate lasted for a while, but Octavian tired of Lepidus, removing him from the triumvirate in 37 BCE. Marc Antony, on the other hand, would fall into a love relationship with Cleopatra, and the two would eventually threaten Rome.

War was declared by Octavian when Antony divorced the former's sister, the marriage having been forced upon him by a decree of the senate five years earlier. The tensions between the two would come to a head when, in a naval battle, Octavian's ships destroyed Marc Antony's navy. Antony, partially thanks to Cleopatra sending her own navy to his aid, would escape the battle, but the two, knowing their fate, committed suicide together[20].

Octavian, now the only member of the triumvirate would be given the name Augustus (meaning dignified or, more obviously, august,) by the senate four years later. It's somewhat unclear exactly when the sole rule of Augustus (formerly Octavian,) would officially begin, but it was definitely in place after he was given his new name. The senate also named him, "The First Citizen of Rome," or princeps. It is from this that we get the term Principate describing this period of emperors.

Although never actually named emperor, Augustus certainly was. Under his sole rule, the territories of Rome would almost double. The undeclared emperor travelled to the expanses of his empire, where he would implement a census in even the farthest reaches of Rome's influence, thereby ensuring that Rome would receive taxes from all of its lands. Augustus is generally considered one of the more benevolent rulers of Rome, as he developed and strengthened infrastructure, instituted the Roman postal service, even fire departments and the city guard of Rome

---

[20] This, incidentally, would be the end of the Egyptian pharaohs. Cleopatra was the last. Shakespearian, ain't it?

(the Praetorian Guard) among other such accomplishments.

He also established that the role of emperor was to be passed down through heredity. When Augustus named Tiberius his successor, he did so hesitantly. Tiberius wasn't a popular man. He was seen as a looming, dark figure who kept to himself to such a degree that people just assumed he was up to no good. Whether Tiberius was a good man misunderstood, or the tyrant that Suetonius and Tacitus wrote in their histories will be more closely examined in the following chapter. Suffice it to say that Tiberius made even Augustus Caesar, the first of the Roman emperors, nervous. In order for Augustus to ease his own mind about the future of Rome, he persuaded Tiberius to name, as his own successor, Germanicus, Tiberius's son and a very well-liked man.

Augustus died in the year 14 CE, after having reunited the lands and the people of Rome and, though expanding the territories dramatically, had secured the new empire. Rome was at peace. He ruled from 27 BCE-14 CE.

Tiberius (14-37 CE)

Tiberius Claudius Nero[21] was the stepson of Augustus. He was so favored by his new stepfather that he was eventually adopted as the son of Augustus, at this point taking the name Tiberius Julius Caesar. This makes things a bit weird when you consider that Tiberius had also married Augustus's daughter.

Regardless, he was a successful general and a remarkably humble man. He was declared the successor to Augustus, despite his rather bold assertions that he wanted nothing to do with the office. In fact, he continually tried throughout his rule to allow the senate to take the lead when it came to legislation. Unfortunately, the die was cast and, by this time, even the senate wanted an emperor to control it. Tiberius is famously credited as having said that the senate was made up of men fit to be slaves.

Through his "I'd really rather not," approach to the office of emperor, Tiberius would often alienate those around him. His detractors, and even many of his supporters, thought him uncaring when he shrugged off some of the perks and powers of his station.

When legions stationed in Germania and Pannonia became mutinous, having waited too long for the bonuses they were promised by Augustus, Tiberius would have to act, however. He sent his son, Drusus Julius Caesar and Tiberius Claudius Nero, Tiberius's

---

[21] Not *that* Nero; he'll come later.

nephew, better known by the name Germanicus to put down the mutiny. The two, however, had different plans.

Instead of quieting the mutiny by force, Germanicus told the riotous soldiers to join him in conquering the neighboring lands, promising them that whatever they laid their hands on during the campaign would be their bonuses. This worked beautifully: The mutiny was quieted, Rome gained some territory and greater fortune.

Tiberius was accused of ordering the murder of his son Germanicus by poisoning. Germanicus had a bright future ahead of him. After his work with the mutineers, Germanicus received a triumph, and was given rule over the east of the Roman Empire. He would be dead within a year. It's possible that Germanicus simply became ill, but he denounced the governor Gnaeus Calpurnius Piso of Syria as having poisoned him.

The governor was arrested and put before the courts. What he did while on trial is cause for speculation, as he warned that he would implicate the emperor himself in the death of Germanicus. Whether Piso was just trying to get himself out of an incredibly sticky situation by dropping the big name, was attempting to cause Tiberius to step in and stop the trial or if the emperor actually did have something to do with Germanicus's death is unclear. Piso, upon realizing that he wasn't going to get reprieve through any means, killed himself. This scandal would stick with Tiberius for the rest of his life, but it wouldn't be the only indignity to be levied against him.

Tiberius would spend much of his time—as much as possible—outside of Rome, delegating much of his responsibilities to the personal secretariat left behind by Augustus. One of the members of the secretariat was named Lucius Aelius Sejanus. Tiberius moved to Capri in 39 CE, leaving Sejanus, a longtime servant of Rome, as an appointed consul in charge of the day-to-day decisions in Rome. As the old saying goes, "Give them an inch and they'll want a mile."

Sejanus almost immediately began taking action to make his position permanent. He installed senators loyal to him and removed senators that might question his authority. He sent Germanicus's widow and two of her sons, Nero and Drusus, into exile and killed most of the rest of the family[22], though some sources say that Tiberius himself was behind all of this. In fact, both the historians Tacitus and Suetonius assert that it was Tiberius himself who imprisoned Aggripina, Germanicus's widow, and the two sons. These sources maintain that much of what he attributed to Sejanus's treachery was simply Tiberius trying to make someone else take the fall for his deeds. What it's certain that Sejanus did himself,

---

[22] Although, Caligula was a notable survivor.

however, was try to cozy up to the Julian family—the direct relatives of Julius Caesar—it's assumed, to garner their support should he attempt to claim sole consulship or regent of Tiberius.

Meanwhile, stories started flying about exactly what Tiberius was up to in Capri. The historian Suetonius would write that the emperor was involved with pedophilia and myriad other sexual debaucheries, although this is sometimes disputed as residual belief from Sejanus's purported treachery. The truth is, we don't really know what Tiberius was doing, but the accusations would stick in the minds of the Romans, causing a great deal of enmity toward the emperor.

Sejanus's plot to overthrow Tiberius was soon discovered and the power-hungry consul was brought to trial before the senate. Here is where Tiberius finally issued a clear and direct order: He ordered Sejanus's execution. This was carried out and Sejanus would die the next week.

Here's where Tiberius's already shaky reputation would become full-on infamy. It was said that Tiberius went on a rampage of treason trials directed at anyone even remotely suspected of complicity with Sejanus. He would order the execution of each and every individual who was even denounced by one of his or her enemies, or loosely associated with the murdered, would-be usurper. This, however, is heavily disputed as records during the time show that only about fifty people were tried for treason during the entirety of Tiberius's rule. Of that number, nearly half were acquitted.

The most we know about Tiberius after he left for Capri is that we don't know much with certainty. Both Suetonius and Tacitus, another historian, also a senator, born during the rule of Nero, state that Tiberius was a mad tyrant with repulsive and criminal sexual appetites and a penchant for killing those whom he suspected of plotting against him. Still, other records don't support the accusations made against Tiberius. We may never know if he was simply a misunderstood, so withdrawn that people would believe just about anything about him, but generally decent ruler or a lecherous, power mad monster. We have a clearer picture of the emperor to follow him, though.

Caligula (37-41 CE)

Gaius Julius Caesar Augustus Germanicus, better known by his derisive nickname Caligula (meaning "little boots"[23],) is probably the most infamous of all the Roman emperors, though he would reign for less than four years before being killed by his own soldiers.

---

[23] He received the nickname as a child when he would accompany his father in military campaigns. The moniker came from the boy's penchant for dressing in a uniform made just for him, right down to the little boots. Almost makes you like the guy until you remember who he became.

The truth is, however, that things may very well have been different for Caligula, had his upbringing not been full of such incredible torment. As you'll remember from the previous section, his mother was banished by Tiberius, or Sejanus, depending on which figure was telling the truth. While his mother was imprisoned during her banishment, she would starve to death.

Caligula's older brothers, Drusus and Nero, would suffer fates all too similar to that of their mother. One, Drusus, was simply locked in a dungeon and denied food. He would starve to death after being without sustenance so long that he began eating the stuffing from his mattress. Nero's fate may have been quicker than that of his brother and mother, but it was no less harsh. Imprisoned, Nero was made to kill himself.

Caligula's father, Germanicus, who had been such a hero to the young emperor-to-be, had died, suspecting that Tiberius had poisoned him, and it was for speaking out about this publicly that his mother and two older brothers would be sent to their deaths.

Now orphans, Caligula and his sisters would go to live with their great grandmother, Augustus's widow, Livia. After her death, they would be passed off to their grandmother, Antonia. These children, however, were largely ignored by their caretakers. It was when

Caligula and his sister, Drusilla, were teenagers that they were said to have secretly become lovers. This would be the first tale of Caligula's perversion, but it would be far from the last.

Fast-forward to 31 BCE, Caligula was sent for by his grand uncle, then Emperor of Rome, Tiberius. The emperor was on the island of Capri at this point, and whether he'd had anything to do with the death of Germanicus or not, that is certainly what Caligula believed about him. The young emperor-to-be couldn't show his animosity for Tiberius, however, forcing him to stifle his cold hatred while the emperor basked in his home away from Rome.

During this time, the Caligula that Rome would come to know for his perversions and his brutality would start showing his colors. One of his favorite past times throughout his rule as emperor was that of watching people being tortured. This dark interest would take hold on Capri, likely as an outlet for the hatred that he could never show Tiberius. He lived a hedonistic life of sex and gluttony. Tiberius once said in regard to his grand-nephew, "I am nursing a viper for the Roman people."

Tiberius would name, not only Caligula as his heir, but also his own grandson, Gemellus. It's been theorized that he may have done this in order to allow the senate, after his death, to decide which of the two would be the better emperor. On the other hand, though, Tiberius was quoted as having said that Caligula would no doubt kill Gemellus, and then someone else would kill Caligula.

Tiberius died in the year 37 CE after being terribly ill for about a month before. Caligula would later be suspected of murdering his grand-uncle; however, it's unclear whether or not this is the case.

What we do know is that the still-young Caligula would be named the new Emperor of Rome. The people were thrilled that Tiberius's reign had ended and saw in Caligula, the image of his father: The brilliant and well-loved Germanicus.

Despite what one may think, the first eight months or so of Caligula's reign were that of a just, even kind ruler. He freed people who were thought to have been imprisoned unfairly by his grand-uncle and would even host a number of public events to improve the morale of the public. Notably, he adopted Gemellus, his co-heir, ensuring that the latter would succeed him upon his own death. These included gladiatorial events, plays and other events, but most notably, included his favorite sport of all: Chariot racing; more on that in a minute.

He was turning out to be a pretty good emperor. That is, until he became deathly ill eight months into his reign. Suetonius writes that the emperor was between life and death. It's also been suggested that he underwent a nervous breakdown. When he recovered from his illness, something inside of him had snapped. This is when his three years of terror would begin.

Among his more infamous acts were forcing parents to watch the execution of their sons, he revamped his love of watching people be tortured and, Suetonius writes, he would spend hours in front of a mirror, practicing making horrific faces. The emperor was mad. His political rivals often met various, but always horrible ends. He was also said to have senators and their wives over for meals, only to pick one of the senators' wives, brutalize her, and then come back and tell the husband all about it. Among the first to be executed by Caligula's order was Gemellus, his adopted son and chosen heir. Caligula had gone mad.

As mentioned before, Caligula's favorite sport was horse racing, and he had a favorite horse. This horse was named Incitatus, meaning quick or swift. Caligula, Suetonius tells us, was so enamored with this horse that he had a stable made of marble constructed for it, and that the night before a race, Caligula would station guards around Incitatus's stable, that were given orders to slay anyone who disturbed the horse's sleep. What was said to have really incensed the senate, though was that Caligula stated that he was going to make the horse a consul. These last stories, if true, may very well have been simply a part of Caligula's rather odd sense of humor, rather than just another sign of the emperor's madness. It's been disputed in recent years whether the stories about Incitatus, and even of Caligula himself, were colored, not so much by actual fact of history, but by the time in which Suetonius wrote his histories, though I doubt we'll ever really know.

Eventually, though, Rome would so tire of Caligula—even those closest to him[24]—that he was assassinated by the Praetorian Guard. He was stabbed thirty times. Now, with two emperors in a row that were utterly despised by the Roman people for their cruelty, they decided to install someone from the same family. Denial, as the story of Caligula would indicate, is often a landmark of powerful societies.

Claudius (41-54 CE)

Claudius was a rather awkward man. Within his family, he usually took the brunt of jokes. When he was much younger, he had suffered a severe illness which left him somewhat disfigured. Despite how his family felt about him, though, after Caligula's death, Claudius was made emperor. Interestingly enough, Claudius was actually put in charge by the Praetorian Guard: The same protectors of Rome who had murdered his predecessor.

---

[24] Caligula was said to tell his wife (and various mistresses,) every time they kissed, "And this beautiful throat will be cut whenever I please." — Suetonius

Claudius, unlike his predecessor, however, would be a good ruler, despite his horrible choice in spouses (we'll get to that in a moment.) Along with expanding the rights and privileges of women, Claudius would improve the court system, he was a gifted historian, and went so far as to institute laws and policies that protected ill and injured slaves.

What Claudius is best known for, and what made him even more popular than anything else among the Roman people of the time was that he actually conquered Britain. As you'll remember, Julius Caesar had astounded Rome by even heading military campaigns that far north. Claudius won Britain by sending some 40,000 troops, along with cavalry and war elephants, across the channel to Britain. The "barbarians," as the Romans referred to them, fought until the last, but the overwhelming force of the Romans finally won the day for Rome. Along with this, he also established "client-kingdoms" which were headed by local kings and/or queens, but swore fealty to Rome. Without these client-kingdoms, it's highly unlikely that Claudius would have been so successful.

Claudius had far exceeded expectations, but not everyone was on his side, most notably, his wives. Messalina, Claudius's wife, had a proclivity toward lavish spending and "spending her nights" with Claudius's servants. So long as Messalina kept her dalliances with the servants, it seems that Claudius simply ignored them. It was when she began an affair with a noble, a man named Gaius Silius, that Claudius became more concerned with the situation.

As the servants posed no threat of claiming the emperorship, they were of no real threat to Claudius politically. Silius, on the other hand, posed a threat to Claudius's rule. As the story goes, Claudius was finally pressed by his advisors to do something about Silius and his wife's affair, so Claudius had Silius killed. After this happened Messalina, fearing her own life, sought refuge in the home of one of her personal friends. While we know what happened next, Claudius's role is disputed. What we do know is that when Claudius was informed that Messalina had been killed, he didn't bother asking the nature of her death, but simply told his servants to bring more wine.

Messalina wouldn't be the end of Claudius's troubles, however, as his next wife, his niece Agrippina, would prove to be the downfall of the emperor himself.

Agrippina, more concerned with the future than the present, was dead set on having her son Nero become the next emperor. To ensure this, she started by pressuring her husband the emperor to have a writer and philosopher named Seneca brought out of his exile. He had originally been cast out by Claudius himself for having an affair with the emperor's niece, Julia Livilla. Claudius, always wanting to please, acquiesced and Seneca became the private tutor of Nero. Agrippina also had Claudius renounce Britannica, his son, and Agrippina continued to systematically get rid of anyone who might prove to be a rival to her son Nero.

When it appeared that Nero was prepared to take rule, Agrippina acted quickly. There are somewhat different versions of what happened next in Cassius Dio's, Suetonius's and Tacitus's writings, but they both have the same result: The death of Claudius.

Claudius was having dinner and was presented with a mushroom, either alone or mixed in with his other food. This mushroom, naturally, was poisonous. Depending on the version, Claudius was either presented with the mushroom by Agrippina herself, or his own personal food tester (the guy whose job it was to prevent this exact thing from happening.) He consumed the mushroom and became very ill.

Depending on the version of the story, at this point, either Claudius died, or was attended to by a doctor. In the latter version of the story, Claudius fell gravely ill after eating the mushroom, but slowly began to recover. This was something Agrippina couldn't abide, and so she persuaded the doctor through unknown means to finish the emperor off by taking a dart, dipped in poison, and forcing it down Claudius's throat.

The final theory on the death of Claudius is that he simply ate the wrong kind of mushroom. Thinking the cap to be safe for consumption, he unwittingly swallowed a type of mushroom commonly referred to as "the death cap." This final theory is unlikely, however, as emperors of this time had already come to expect assassination attempts. In order to prevent such an occurrence, there would be one or more servants whose job was to taste any food or drink that was given to the emperor. If the servant lived, the emperor would dine. If the servant died, well, you get the idea.

Regardless, Claudius, a truly popular and comparatively good ruler was killed. Agrippina would get her wish: Her son, Nero, would become emperor.

Nero (54-68 CE)

Lucius Domitius Ahenobarbus, Agrippina's son, was named emperor of Rome after presenting a eulogy for his lost adoptive father, Claudius, before the Roman Senate. Upon completion of this eulogy, he was named emperor, and he donned the moniker Nero Claudius Caesar Augustus Germanicus.

It was commonplace for emperors to change their names, as you've seen, and the names they chose were largely similar. The reason for this was an early form of public relations. It wouldn't be wise for an emperor to take the name Caligula, however, the name Caesar was necessary in order to implant the idea of the new emperor's right to rule. Augustus, the first true emperor of Rome had also been a very popular leader and so this name was also common. Germanicus, who was supposed to be the successor of Tiberius, had also been well loved by the people. Finally, as Claudius was the surname of the emperor from whom Nero had gained his heirship, he took this name as well, although this final was already in place when Claudius adopted him.

Nero is one of Rome's more scandalous emperors, only outdone in his infamy by Caligula. Although most have heard the story of the burning of Rome, Nero's reign actually began reasonably benign. Due to the input of his advisors, specifically Seneca, and the leader of the Praetorian Guard named Burrus.

Some of Nero's early dictates included such things as lowering taxes, did away with secret trials as even he considered them an affront to the law and to the people, he also allowed more power and liberty to the senate, limited the powers of the wealthiest citizens as the income gap had led to the tyranny of the nobles over the common people, made provisions for slaves to bring formal grievances against their masters and he even did away with executions altogether. He was a lover of music, the theater and was a patron of the gladiatorial arena. It would be Nero's love of the arts that would lead to some of his more bizarre acts, and give rise to a myth by which he is still predominantly known.

Although Agrippina had gone to great lengths in order to ensure her son's rule, she and his advisors were not on the best of terms. Seneca and Burrus, often considered as having been the actual rulers of Rome until the year 62, generally steered Nero toward more moderate actions, encouraging the young emperor[25] to rule, not according to what his mother wished, but of his own accord. Feeling her grasp slipping on her son, and thus the empire, Agrippina only became more entrenched and more outspoken about Nero.

One of the things that would most typify Nero's personality was his penchant for women other than his wife. Part of Agrippina's actions to ensure the heirship of Nero was that she convinced Claudius, Nero's adoptive father and actual grand-uncle, to arrange a marriage between Nero and Claudius's daughter, Octavia. Incestuous marriage was very common among the Caesars and other higher-ups within the Roman Empire. Nero, however, had eyes for a former slave named Claudia Acte.

Nero's relationship with Octavia was strained from the outset, largely due to Octavia's inability to provide him with an heir. When he began consorting

---

[25] Nero was 17 when he became emperor.

with Acte, however, tensions rose. Nero had begun threatening to divorce his wife, but this move was unsupported by the public and vehemently opposed by his mother, as the marriage had helped to ensure Nero's rightful reign as emperor. The emperor, however, wouldn't simply let the matter drop, however, and began publicly referring to Acte as his wife.

Due to her grip over her son having been all but severed, Agrippina actually began to champion Claudius's son, Britannica, who she had pushed out of the way only a few years earlier, as the rightful ruler of Rome. This threat wouldn't live long, however, as in the year 55, Britannica mysteriously died. The mystery may not be too great, however, as Britannica died the day before he was to be considered an adult, and thus a true contender and threat against Nero. Although the emperor denied involvement, stating that Britannica had died after having a terrible seizure, it's generally accepted that Nero either killed his rival personally or had him murdered.

After his affair with Acte ended, Nero would then take, as his mistress, a married noblewoman named Poppaea Sabina. While such a thing was generally tolerated of the Roman Emperors, Nero's renewal of his threat to divorce Octavia remained incredibly unpopular. His mother Agrippina continued her public denouncement of her son's actions.

Tired of his mother's constant, and often public, opposition, Nero had Agrippina killed in the year 59. It was at this point that Nero would go from the admittedly promiscuous emperor that was still generally loved by the people for his progressive reforms, into the vicious tyrant that he would be known for throughout history.

Nero had long wanted to be with his newest love-interest, Sabina, but was unable to simply divorce her. He first had her removed from the palace, and then he had her banished. These measures were extremely unpopular, though. Finally, Nero decided that it would be easier just to have her killed, as the public tends to have an extremely short memory and, with Octavia out of their minds, she would simply be forgotten. He was right.

Nero had Octavia killed in 62 CE, and without her actual presence to remind them that they liked her, the people quickly forgot about her, at least in a practical sense. What really started to bother the masses was the way that Nero publicly aired his artistic interests[26]. His various performances, both musical and theatrical were considered far beneath his station, and it would be here that the people of Rome would really start to have a problem with him. This enmity

---

[26] A good corollary is in modern populations becoming outraged in regard to sex scandals, but remaining relatively silent about genocide and war crimes committed by their own leaders or the leaders of other nations.

of the public toward Nero would only grow from then on out.

His self-indulgence had already soured many of Rome's people, but his most lavish spending came when he decided that he wanted to put on these public performances. It's said that he was even considering abdicating the emperorship in order to pursue a career in the arts, but he never went so far as to actually do this.

Things had come to a head in the year 62 CE when his two advisors were no longer around; Burrus had died and Seneca retired. It was after this that Nero divorced Octavia and had her killed, accusing her of infidelity. This accusation not only was false, but it was so widely known to be false that even under torture, those close to Octavia maintained that she had always remained faithful to her husband.

The masses had turned on Nero, many even going so far as to accuse him of treason. Nero, who had previously abolished the death penalty, began executing or exiling anyone who he saw to be a political threat. He also began plans for what would be his greatest project: the Domus Aurea[27] or, in English, the Golden House. This was to be a It was with the Great Fire,

---

[27] For those of you who have ever wondered why gold's symbol on the periodic table is Au, this is why.

however, that what was left of Nero's popularity would collapse.

The Great Fire of Rome is the single event for which Nero is best known, although in reality, he had nothing to do with it. The fire started in the stores at the southeastern end of the Circus Maximus (literally: Great Circle,) and would burn for ten days, consuming an estimated 75% of Rome.

Nero, about 35 miles away, in Antium, at the start of the fire, had become so unpopular that he was immediately thought to be the person responsible for the fire. Ostensibly, Nero was said to have played his fiddle while Rome burned. This last is notably false for a couple of reasons. First, as stated above, Nero wasn't even in Rome at the time the fire began. Secondly, while being a lover of music and a musician himself, fiddles hadn't yet been invented.

In truth, once Nero heard about the fire, he immediately raced back to Rome, offering his own private gardens and opened public buildings to shelter displaced and threatened citizens. The people, however, didn't trust Nero, many of them thinking that he had either set the fire himself or had it started. Therefore, in their minds, any aid he was offering was likely a trap of some sort. He actually faced the crisis in a very responsible way, even importing grain to ensure that his people would have enough to eat.

Regardless of Nero's innocence in setting the fire, he did capitalize on its destruction. His Domus Aurea now had plenty of room. In fact, at one point, Nero was said to have planned about half of the space which had been destroyed in the fire, nearly half of Rome itself, for the building. It was after this construction began that many of those who hadn't believed Nero was behind the fire began believing. While this is unlikely to have been a serious plan or, if it was, to have been practical, it only served to lead to his infamy.

Furthermore, he blamed a fledgling cult that was starting to gain some ground among the other cults in Rome for the fire. These people, he often burned alive or famously had thrown to the lions in the gladiatorial arena, although lions were certainly not the only foes these cult members would face. The name of this Roman cult, if you haven't guessed it already, was Christianity. We'll see a lot more about them later.

The estimates for the expanse of the Domus Aureus that *was* constructed ranges from between one-hundred to three-hundred acres. It spanned three of Rome's five foothills and parts of it still stand today, although this is only a small portion of what had once been built. In the middle of the Domus Aureus was a manmade reservoir and through its construction, the Domus Aureus, along with Nero's rebuilding of Rome[28] would effectively drain the Roman treasury.

On a military front, Nero would see some major losses. Though he had attempted to conquer a land called Parthia, a third party between the Roman Empire and the Kingdom of Armenia, this campaign had to be abandoned.

Another military issue that faced Nero was with the newly conquered land of Britain. While Britain had been conquered by Claudius, it would see its first major rebellion during Nero's rule. This occurred within a client kingdom under the rule of King Prasutagus and his wife, Queen Boudicca. Prasutagus had gained his station through a deal with the previous emperor, Claudius. However, Roman soldiers in the area raped Prasutagus and Boudicca's daughters, meanwhile flogging the queen herself, any loyalties the rulers may have had with Rome vanished. While this insurrection was put down, it had been rather successful.

So, with a large portion of the city burnt down (though being rebuilt,) military tragedies, his murder of his mother and first wife and the financial straits which had been caused by the Domus Aurea, Nero became desperate, raised taxes. It would be this final

---

[28] Notably, the manner of reconstruction was not in the classical style of Rome, rather based off of Greek architecture.

act of raising taxes that would be Nero's undoing. Governors began denouncing Nero in favor of others and even his own Praetorian Guard renounced him. In the year 65, there was even an attempt to restore the republic, although this failed miserably. These things weighed heavily on Nero's mind, and when the senate denounced him, even to the extent of declaring him an enemy of the state, the strain proved too much to bear. Nero killed himself on the eighth of June, 68 CE. Supposedly, Nero lacked the courage to kill himself, rather had a slave do the deed, with the famous last words "What an artist dies in me!"

Nero, though often thought to be a cruel and senseless ruler, wasn't as unpopular as it may seem, however. Along with Elvis-esque sightings, varying stories of his suicide led many people to believe that he still lived. One of the emperors to follow him would even go so far as to take Nero's name as part of his imperial moniker. For better or for worse, Nero's reign would spell the end for the Julio-Claudian dynasty of emperors. What would follow, in the short-term, at least, was chaos.

CHAPTER 23

The Principate through Marcus Aurelius

After the death of Nero, Rome was far from fallen; however, it would take a while for the subsequent emperors to regain the control that the Julio-Claudian emperors had.

The Year of Four Emperors (68-69 CE)

Galba

During Nero's reign, his tax policy, necessary to rebuild Rome, had won him many enemies. Among these was a Roman governor in Spain named Servius Sulpicius Galba. The idea of supplanting Nero with Galba originated with another governor, this one named Caius Julius Vindex.

Galba and Vindex corresponded for some time, discussing plans to usurp Nero, placing Galba as emperor. Vindex would lead an unsuccessful revolution in Galba's favor which resulted in Vindex's suicide and the Roman senate declaring Galba an enemy of the state. However, in the year 68 CE, Nero's own Praetorian Guard would denounce the emperor in favor of Galba. Without the support of the Praetorian Guard, Nero's influence as emperor had crumbled. When he fled the city and subsequently killed himself, it would be Galba that took his place.

So, Galba was now to be emperor, but he would have to travel from Hispania to Rome. During this time, the prefect of the Praetorian Guard, Nymphidius Sabinus, made a play to become emperor himself, though he would be killed by his own men.

Galba would finally arrive and take the title of emperor. He was greeted by adoring crowds and high hopes. He didn't, however, provide the many favors that he and others had promised to the Praetorian Guard or to the Germanic legions of Rome. His short reign would be full of executions in an attempt to consolidate his power and overall paranoia. Though Nero was now dead and had been declared an enemy of Rome, some of his reforms were still popular. Galba did away with these. This awkward and violent reign would come to an end when the legions in Germania Inferior swore fealty, not to Galba, but to Marcus Salvius Otho.

Galba tried one last time to solidify his rule as emperor, naming his own successor to be Lucius Calpurnius Piso Licinianus, a senator. This plan backfired, however, and Otho rebelled even more, this time bribing the Praetorian Guard into supporting him. When Galba discovered the plot, he took to the streets of Rome, trying impotently to rally support for himself. When this support never came, Galba met a bitter end at the hands of the Praetorian Guard.

Otho

With Galba now dead, the senate gave the title of emperor to Otho, who had so ambitiously defied the still-warm emperor. Otho's reign would only last three months, as another ambitious man, General Vitellius had declared himself the rightful successor of Galba. This may have been an inconsequential matter if it weren't for the fact that Vitellius had under his command the best of the best among Roman legions.

With little support, though still fresh in office, Otho would attempt to fend off the massive forces of Vitellius, but after a particularly crushing defeat, Otho saw the writing on the wall. With Rome already in a state of upheaval over the rapid succession of emperors, Otho killed himself.

Vitellius

Vitellius, though a powerful general, started his reign with a dubious start. At first, he offended the masses by declaring himself Pontifex Maximus, or high priest, of Rome on a day that, according to Roman superstition, held bad omens. From there, his reign would only grow more self-aggrandizing and violent.

Vitellius held frequent parades and celebrations in his own honor, including three banquets a day. This quickly emptied the Roman treasury, however, and if history tells us anything, it's that you can generally get away with anything but messing with people's cash flow.

To further insulate himself in his role, he would invite political rivals to dine or simply to meet with him, often making them promises of wealth and influence, only to have them killed upon their arrival. Creditors to whom Vitellius owed payment were summarily executed for being so insolent as to ask for the payment that had been promised them.

Vitellius became so unpopular that the Roman armies in the Middle East and in Africa declared a man named Vespasian as their emperor. Vespasian had been sent to Judea in order to quell the Great Jewish Revolt in 67, by then-emperor Nero. Leaving his son Titus in charge of stopping the rebellion, Vespasian travelled to Alexandria, gaining the full support of Egypt and, most importantly, access to its grain reserves.

This started a domino effect as more and more provinces declared Vespasian and not Vitellius as the Emperor of Rome. Although Vespasian was already marching toward Rome, he had a lot of ground to cover before he would arrive. This didn't stop his supporters, however, as Marcus Antonius Primus led the Roman forces of the Danube to invade Italy itself.

Vespasian

Now desperate, Vitellius tried convincing tribes and other local groups to support him, only to be consistently rejected. He bribed people he thought would help him retain power with money and the promise of power within his regime, but it was too little, too late.

He tried sending emissaries, even including a number of the Vestal Virgins to plea for some sort of negotiation, but his ambassadors only returned with news that the armies were now at the gates of Rome. Now unable to deny that his reign had come to an end, Vitellius made plans to leave Rome in order to save his own life. He may have made it if he hadn't insisted on stopping by the palace just one last time. Vespasian's men had already taken the city, and Vitellius was killed on sight. Vespasian was made emperor, even though his men had destroyed the Temple of Jupiter and had invaded Rome. By this time, though, invading Rome was a favorite tactic among those who wished to rule it.

Vespasian was made emperor on December 21, 69, thus being the fourth emperor that year. Despite the constant upheaval of this period, however, Vespasian would go on to rule for thirteen years. He would be the first emperor of a new dynasty: The Flavians.

The Flavian Dynasty

Vespasian (cont'd)

As we saw at the end of the Year of Four Emperors, one of the greatest threats to a sitting emperor lied with armies who were more loyal to their commanders than to the Caesar who was supposed to be their high ruler. One of the first things Vespasian did, and quite possibly why he was relatively unchallenged as the previous emperors had been, made a point to reorganize the army, so that it would become more of a professional institution and more loyal to Rome itself.

Vespasian (reigned 69-79 CE) was also responsible for bringing in learned and wealthy individuals, installing them in the senate. This had become necessary as, during the reign of Nero and the subsequent civil wars of the Year of Four Emperors, senate membership had dropped dramatically, as had its influence. He was a widely popular ruler, although his systematic tax increases, of crucial necessity in order to replenish the treasury after Vitelli's short reign, brought political tension.

Vespasian also started construction on an amphitheater to be named after his family. The Flavian Amphitheater was to be not only enormous in size, but intricate in its design. There were multiple entrances to the floor of the amphitheater where gladiators would do battle, the theater portion itself could be flooded to accommodate naval battles, and there were even trap doors which would allow a beast or gladiator to enter the action in the middle of a fight. Wooden balls would be dropped with various prizes written on them. These could be exchanged for the corresponding items which included things such as gold, clothing and slaves. This enormous amphitheater is known by a different name today: The Colosseum.

Vespasian was the first ruler in many years to die a natural death. Upon becoming ill with the sickness that would take him, he is said to have uttered, "I suppose I shall soon be a god." This is almost certainly a reference to the practice of Roman Emperors being deified upon their deaths.

Titus

Titus (reigned 79-81 CE,) Vespasian's son, would succeed his father as emperor. Titus is most well-known for having successfully quelled the Jewish insurrection. His father, as you'll remember, had left Titus in charge of the front when he, Vespasian, made for Rome in order to become emperor. During his campaign, Titus led the destruction of the Second Temple of Solomon. He finished the construction of the Colosseum, and held the inaugural games: 100 days of gladiators, naval battles, chariot races and other popular attractions of the day.

One of the more important historical events of the time, however, had nothing to do with the emperor: It was during Titus's reign that Mount Vesuvius erupted, covering the Roman city of Pompeii in hot volcanic ash.

Titus, though his reign would only last from 79-81 BCE died a popular emperor. His death was caused by a fever while travelling toward Sabine, though the origin of this fever is disputed among both ancient and modern scholars. Some maintain that Titus was actually killed by his brother, and the next emperor, Domitian, stated to have fed his brother a deadly type of sea-slug, though this is largely discredited. Multiple histories, specifically those of Suetonius and Dio, do state that Titus's death was a natural one, but that his brother, Domitian, had abandoned the emperor as his health quickly deteriorated. His last words were said to be, "I have only made one mistake." The meaning of these words has stirred some debate throughout history, as it's unclear what he may have been referring to. Many maintain that his one mistake was not seeing his brother's treachery while he had the ability to protect himself and the Roman Empire, however, we'll never really know for sure.

Domitian

When Domitian (reigned 81-96 CE,) Titus's brother and also the biological son of Vespasian, assumed the title of emperor, his first act was to have his fallen brother deified. He would later erect the Arco di Tito, the Arch of Titus, in commemoration of his brother's victory in Jerusalem. It's often thought that Domitian's public reverence of Titus was borne of both a guilty conscience and in order to win the people to his side after the death of his brother.

Domitian helped to reinforce the propaganda that had typified the Flavian rule, ensuring that cities both near and far had reminders of who their leaders really were. This came mostly through the use of the emperor's face on coinage, but also consisted of statues, portraits and monuments build either in reverence to or directly of the Flavians.

Domitian would rule Rome for a span of fifteen years. This had become quite the feat as no emperor since Tiberius had ruled as long. His reign, however, was not to end as his father's or his brothers, though.

Domitian, despite his later unpopularity and (spoiler alert) assassination, actually did many great things for Rome, including bolstering the economy by revaluing Roman currency. He would bring the Roman economy back to the heights it had achieved under Augustus. Though he would later have to devalue the currency, even then it held higher value than it had for many years.

He took a bit of a different approach militarily than had his two predecessors, favoring a defensive strategy rather than being so intent on conquering new lands. Despite this, Scotland would come under Roman rule under Domitian, and the Roman territories in the east would also expand. He built forts, numbering 300, in the land of modern-day Germany and surrounding areas. This would strengthen the Roman frontier and protect it from incursion from outside forces.

He rebuilt much of Rome that had been destroyed to one degree or another in the Great Fire, and even finished temples in honor of Titus and Vespasian. He also finished the reconstruction of the Temple of Jupiter.

Where Domitian came into trouble, despite his popularity among the masses of Rome, was in his disempowerment of the senate and his more despotic brand of rule. These political woes are often cited as the reason for Domitian's paranoia and the executions he would carry out. This, however, only hurt him in the long run. The senate had become so enraged at Domitian's marginalization of them, and his willingness to have political threats killed that they had him assassinated in 96 CE. They declared him an enemy of Rome the following day.

Nerva and the Transition to the Antonine Dynasty

The first ruler to follow Domitian would be known as the first of the five good emperors. He was named Nerva (ruled 96-98 CE.) His appointment was a political move on the part of the senate, as he was already 69 years old and had no children to name as heirs. The senate regained much of its power, and the illusion of republic was born again, though it would never return in reality. Nerva was a fine emperor who led Rome with a balanced budget; however, he was unpopular with the military, particularly the Praetorian Guard. This disfavor led to a mutiny that was only quelled when the emperor named, as his successor, Trajan, a very popular general of the time.

Nerva's reign ended with his death in 98 CE, caused by a stroke. His successor would begin the next dynasty of emperors in Rome.

Trajan and the Beginning of the Antonine Dynasty

Nerva's successor, Trajan (ruled 98-117 CE,) would become a popular and long-ruling emperor. He ruled longer than anyone had since Augustus and Tiberius, and despite the Roman proclivity for ousting its leaders, there aren't recorded uprisings during Trajan's reign.

He was considered the first soldier-emperor of Rome. That is, he gained power directly through virtue of his command of an army. Trajan actually stayed on the Roman frontiers for about a year after being named emperor. He was famous for bringing the standing army up to a massive strength of thirty legions, and would conquer the lands of Dacia and would lead a campaign against Parthia. Unlike Domitian, Trajan enjoyed a relatively positive relationship with the senate. This, in spite of his rather despotic rule, was accomplished by being cordial and diplomatic with the senators rather than reviling them.

It would be his conquest of Dacia that would bring vast amounts of new wealth and an undeniable sense of renewed vigor within the Roman Empire. These two wars against Dacia, one in 101, the other which ended in Roman conquest in 106, is immortalized in Trajan's Column[29], an enormous pillar with an intricate pictorial description of the wars and of Trajan's victory.

---

[29] This is a fascinating look at Trajan's column from National Geographic: http://www.nationalgeographic.com/trajan-column/

Trajan led many successful military campaigns, and focused largely on bolstering food stores and increasing security. It was during Trajan's rule that the words, "Two things only the people anxiously desire — bread and circuses[30]," were written by the satirist Juvenal. This, of course, isn't to imply that there were no other concerns facing the empire, rather, that times were so relatively peaceful and prosperous within Rome that the populous was largely complacent.

Trajan remained popular throughout his rule. Parents who were unable to financially support their children were provided with financial assistance under Trajan's rule and citizens who were considered to have been unfairly imprisoned by Domitian were released. Trajan built many roads, bridges and aqueducts and is widely known for building a temple which would be dedicated to all of the gods. He died in August of 117, due to a long-term illness that led to a stroke.

Hadrian

Hadrian (ruled 117-138 CE) was the adopted son of Trajan and the next emperor of Rome. He would later be known as the third in the period of five good emperors.

---

[30] Circus refers to the place where horse races and gladiatorial events took place. The term simply means circle and describes the physical characteristics of the locale.

Like Trajan, Hadrian was well known for the building projects completed during his rule. With Hadrian, however, this legacy extended beyond monuments or infrastructure to include the construction of cities throughout the expanse of the Roman Empire and, most famously, the Vallum Hadriani: Hadrian's Wall.

This wall was constructed in Britain and was begun when Hadrian visited the region. The wall was massive[31], stretching from the east coast of Britain to the west coast, demarcating the northernmost boundary of the Roman Empire, all told, some seventy-three miles long.

Hadrian spent much of his reign, an estimated twelve of his twenty-one year rule, outside the walls of Rome itself. He inspected outposts, met with military commanders, visited and toured many of Rome's provinces and generally ensured the strength and fortitude of Rome's various frontiers and regions.

Hadrian died in 138 CE, but not before appointing his next two successors: Antoninus Pius and Marcus Aurelius. Antoninus Pius was only named heir after Hadrian had ensured that the former would adopt Marcus Aurelius and name him as the successor of the same. These two rulers would be the final two of the period of five good emperors.

---

[31] Much, though far from all of it, remains today.

Antoninus Pius

Pius (reigned 138-161 CE) was a philosophic and even-tempered ruler. Under his guidance, Rome would withstand the onslaught of Germanic hordes, pacified an attack from the Britons, quelled a number of rebellions and would see the construction of the Wall of Antoninus in Britain. This he did without leaving the walls of Rome.

He was very much Hadrian's successor, leaving his predecessor's appointees at their stations and having Hadrian deified. He was, if anything, more generous than even Hadrian had been. He gave money to his soldiers and to his citizens, and lent further monies at very low interest rates. He would even go so far as to advocate for the protection of slaves against unjust treatment by their masters. He built and rebuilt aqueducts, bathhouses and oversaw the construction of the Temple of Hadrian.

Although there was a lot of military activity during his reign in various parts of the empire, Antoninus's reign was marked by a period of relative peace. His rule would be second in length only to that of Augustus himself.

He died in the year 161, reportedly after over indulging in a meal of cheese that had caused him a great fever. His successor, Marcus Aurelius, would be the last of the five good emperors.

Marcus Aurelius

Marcus Aurelius (reigned 161-180 CE) is and was best known for his philosophies. He wrote The Meditations[32], a text containing his personal thoughts and approaches to Stoic philosophy.

His reign was to be beset by even more conflict, especially with Parthia over the land of Armenia. Rome would win this conflict, but Armenia would change hands many times as the Romans and the Parthians continued to do battle.

The other major threat, one which would bring back not-so-fond memories, was with the Germanic tribes at the northeast of the Roman Empire. These would come to be called the Marcomannic Wars, and they would last from 166-180 CE. Rome would emerge victorious, but the long years of war had taken a toll on the armies of Rome.

Marcus Aurelius, however, would remain popular throughout his rule, which ended with his death the same year that Rome won the Marcomannic Wars: 180 CE.

It's interesting to note that Marcus Aurelius had a co-emperor, his adoptive brother and biological son of

---

[32] This text is still available for purchase.

Antoninus Pius, named Lucius Verus. Verus joined Marcus Aurelius on the campaigns against the Parthians and, before his death due to plague, in the Marcomannic Wars. It was Marcus Aurelius himself that ensured the co-rule, refusing to take the title of emperor unless Verus, the biological son of Pius, ruled alongside him.

With Marcus Aurelius's death came the end of the five good emperors. What would follow would begin a steady decline, leading to the Third Century Crisis and not long after, the fall of Rome. Marcus Aurelius's son, Commodus, was installed as emperor after the former's death, but he would not be anywhere near the emperor his father was.

Commodus

Commodus (177-192 CE) was a strange man and an even stranger emperor. While it wasn't uncommon for the nobility, even the emperors themselves to be fans of gladiatorial games and attend them regularly, Commodus wasn't content just watching; more on that shortly.

You may have noticed that there are a few years of overlap with the rule of Marcus Aurelius and Commodus. During this period, ending with Marcus Aurelius's death, the two reigned as co-emperors. Commodus and his father journeyed to the distant battle fronts and, for a time, the two seemed to be on the same page. When his father passed in the year 180, however, things would quickly deteriorate in Rome.

Only two years into his sole reign, Commodus's own sister, Lucilla, met with some of Rome's senators, conspiring with them to see her brother, the emperor, assassinated. While he spared Lucilla's life (for a little while anyway,) he had the conspirators killed, starting with Quintianus, his nephew and the one who wielded the dagger in the failed assassination attempt.

Motives for this attempt are debatable, though the most popular theory is that Lucilla had grown envious of Commodus's wife, Bruttia Crispina[33]. Another, and not necessarily contradictory theory, is that Commodus had never really taken his duties as emperor seriously, passing off his responsibilities to his trusted advisors, leaving himself to pursue his fantasies.

It was said of Commodus that he was not intrinsically a vicious or a bad man, but that he was, put bluntly, rather stupid. He had neither taste nor patience for governance, and so was consistently supplanted by the advisors to whom he gave power over the day-to-day operations of Rome. His gullibility, along with the

---

[33] Fans of the movie Gladiator will note the reversed role in this particular instance between the Hollywood version and the historical version of events here.

actual plots against him and his famous cowardice led Commodus to become wildly paranoid.

It wasn't until he was betrayed by one advisor, Saoterus's successor, Perennis, and forced to execute the next, Cleander, in order to appease a riotous mob on his own doorstep, that Commodus would deign to take rule back into his own hands.

It's possible that the odd nature of his return to rule was how he believed he would become safe: Through fear. In reality, though, his actions simply appeared strange. He took to wearing a lion's skin over his head, as the mythical Hercules had after defeating the Numean Lion[34], and carrying a club. He went so far as to have the senate declare him a living god and he began insisting that people not call him Commodus, but Hercules, the son of Zeus. As if that wasn't enough, he began entering the Colosseum, facing his opponents—usually either disabled slaves or animals—from a raised platform, thereby ensuring that he would always win.

Whether he did this to give would-be assassins the impression that he was not to be trifled with, or because he had, quite simply, lost it is unclear, but this last act, that of entering the Colosseum as a gladiator, was seen as an affront to his station.

---

[34] See Discovering Ancient Greece.

During this period of his rule, Rome would, again, fall prey to a massive fire. Commodus rebuilt much of Rome. Commodus declared that he hadn't merely rebuilt Rome, however, but that he had re-founded it. He renamed the city and its people after himself, calling the city Colonia Lucia Annia Commodiana, its citizens, Commodiani. He also renamed the months of the calendar after himself, his many titles and the various grandiosities that he believed himself to be. His megalomania truly knew no bounds, and in the year 191, he had his own wife, Crispina, banished and subsequently executed.

Things finally came to a head when, after dictating yet another of his many lists of people to be executed, he announced that he was going to compete in the gladiatorial games in celebration of the "re-founding," those closest to him had had enough. His mistress, Marcia, brought him his wine; however, this wine had been poisoned. Alternately, it was his food which was poisoned. Commodus would survive the initial attempt, vomiting the poison before it caused fatal damage, but his equivalent to a personal trainer, a professional wrestler[35] named Narcissus would finish the emperor off, strangling him to death.

With the fall of Commodus, the empire had undergone yet another great change. It had experienced a great, if not unprecedented, period of general peace

[35] Not in the modern sense, rather a Greco-Roman wrestler by profession.

and prosperity, but Commodus had, in the space of his reign, undone much of the good that had been put in place. What would follow would be yet another series of civil wars and, while Rome would appear to stabilize for a time, after Marcus Aurelius's death, it would only be a matter of time before the empire would fall.

CHAPTER 24

The Fall of the Republic and the Rise of the Caesars

At this point, it's of much greater use to focus more on the specific events of Rome than its rulers. While these will still be discussed, the historical events leading to the downfall of the Roman Empire, culminating in the sack of Rome by the Visigoths in the fifth century BCE, are of greater import and so will be discussed at greater length.

The exact date of Rome's fall is often debated, however, the Western Empire, that is, the empire that actually included Rome, would fall to foreign rule in the year 476 AD. By this time, however, Roman might had already been greatly fractured and it was the Eastern Empire, commonly known as the Byzantine Empire that would hold true power. While the first great blow came with the Third Century Crisis, the civil wars preceding even this period, beginning after the death of Commodus, wreaked havoc within the Roman Empire.

As it was before Vespasian reclaimed the peace of Rome, it would be many ambitious men who would lead to the weakening of Rome and the civil wars in the year after Commodus's death. This period was called the Year of the Five Emperors.

Civil War and the Year of the Five Emperors

As we've seen, Roman history is rife with ruthless men who saw themselves as the only natural ruler of Rome. In the year 193 CE, the empire would see five such men: Pertinax, Didius Julianus, Pescennius Niger, Clodius Albinus and Septimius Severus.

Commodus hadn't named a successor, therefore, everyone with any remote claim to power assumed that they were next in line. The first to take the rule was Pertinax. He was a fair ruler in most aspects, however, he had revoked the special treatment that Commodus had given the soldiers and the Praetorian Guard. He also had to contend with suspicion of complicity in Commodus's murder and the massive deficit his predecessor had left him, but it was the above treatment of the army that would be Pertinax's downfall. He was killed at the hands of the Praetorian Guard in March.

The next in line was Didius Julianus. He competed for the senate's favor, finally gaining it by promising to pay the armies more than his political rival had offered. Like Pertinax, however, Julianus was suspected of having participated, either through planning, commission or both, in his predecessor's murder. Because of this, two new rivals would arise to take advantage of the situation. The first, Septimus Severus, simply pronounced himself as Emperor of Rome less than two weeks after the death of Pertinax. The second, Pescennius Niger, was sought by the citizens of Rome who feared Julianus due to the accusations levied against him.

Niger, heeding the call of the Roman citizens would also declare himself emperor. He and Severus would do battle in the coming years, however, victory wouldn't come until yet another man, Clodius Albinus, was approached by Severus. Albinus had originally refused the offer to become emperor after Commodus's death, but when approached by Severus with a deal that would, albeit temporarily, grant the former the title of emperor. Due to Albinus's acceptance of this role, which also increased his personal reach over the territories of the empire after stepping down in Severus's favor, Severus was eventually able to defeat Niger.

Upon his return from battle, Severus would take control of Rome. He ensured this position by having Julianus killed, though the order of execution was actually made by the senate. Although he had defeated two of his foes, that wasn't enough for Severus. He began a new civil war, this time against Albinus. At the completion of this successful campaign, Severus would come through the other side as Caesar and rightful ruler of Rome.

The role of emperor over the coming years would often be shared. Severus (ruled 193-211 CE) was co-emperor with his successor, Caracalla (ruled 198-217 CE) and also with Geta (ruled 209-211 CE.) Caracalla had Geta killed and Caracalla's successor, Macrinus (ruled 217-218 CE) would have *him* killed. Of this group, only Severus escaped assassination.

This wasn't the end of the infighting, though. Both Macrinus and his son, Diadumenian (ruled 217-218 CE) were killed so that Elagabalus (reigned 218-222 CE) could ascend to rule. Elagabalus was killed, this time not by another would-be emperor, but by the Praetorian Guard who, it can only be assumed, had started to grow wistful for the times that it was them who killed an emperor.

Severus Alexander, Elagabalus's successor would actually maintain rule for thirteen years (222-235 CE,) but this period of massive upheaval had taken its toll, and the empire was about to undergo a radical change from which it would never recover.

The Crisis of the Third Century

Severus Alexander had ruled for a while, but he had hardly stabilized Rome. So much of Rome's time and resources were spent, destroyed or otherwise nullified through the years of rapid succession and usurpation. There was a huge economic downturn and the aftermath of the civil wars. It was when Severus Alexander was murdered by his own army that things really started to plummet, however.

Those with aspirations of seizing the Roman Empire weren't done fighting among each other. After numerous attempts and threats of invasion and the exacerbating factor of widespread disease added to the economic depression and the fractured alliances of the still-recent civil wars, the Third Century Crisis had begun.

If the claims to the role of Caesar in the previous section weren't bad enough, between the years of 235-285 CE, over two dozen emperors would be officially accepted by the senate, with about forty-one individuals declaring themselves as emperor.

While this is good information to have, I'll try to make this quick as it is rather convoluted:

Maximinus I (ruled March 235-June 238 CE) was declared emperor in 235 CE, only to be killed by the Praetorian Guard in 238 CE.

Gordian I and his son, Gordian II (ruled March 22, 238-April 12, 238) were declared emperor while Maximinus was still emperor, though their claim would only last three weeks. Gordian II was killed in battle and his father killed himself that same day upon hearing the news of his son. Maximus would still be emperor for about two more months before his death at the hands of the Praetorian Guard.

Pupienus and Balbinus ("ruled" April 22, 238-July 29, 238 CE) were quickly declared co-emperors ten days after the death of the Gordians but, though they would outlive Maximinus I, they, too would be killed by the Praetorian Guard.

Gordian III (ruled 238-244 CE) was also a co-ruler with Pupienus and Balbinus, installed on the same day, but would outlive his fellow emperors until his death—cause unknown—in 244.

Phillip I (ruled 244-249 CE) would succeed Gordian III, and install his own son Phillip II in 247 CE. The reign of Phillip I and Phillip II would end when Trajan Decius would kill Phillip I in 249.

Trajan Decius (ruled 249-251 CE) and his son, whom he installed as co-emperor in 251, were actually not killed by Romans, but by Goths at the Abrittus in June of 251.

Hostilian (ruled June 251-a few months later, 251 CE) would become the next emperor. At this same time, Trebonianus Gallus (ruled June 251-August 253 CE) was installed, not as co-emperor, but as a rival emperor (still of Rome, still given the same title.) Hostilian would die of an epidemic later that year. Gallus would install his own son, Volusianus, as co-emperor around the time of Hostilian's death.

Gallus and Volusianus were killed by their own troops in 253, in order to place Aemilian (August-October 253 CE) into the role of Caesar. He was killed two months later by *his* own troops in order to place Valerian (253-260 CE) at the head of the empire.

Valerian would actually rule for about seven years, dying in captivity after being captured by Persians in the Battle of Edessa. During all of this time of infighting, Rome's enemies hadn't simply stepped back to let the Romans get things figured out. In fact, during all of this upheaval, the civil wards were met with wars and skirmishes from outside forces. Valerian's death was to be a humiliation of Rome at the hands of the Persians. After Valerian's capture, it's said that the Persian King, Shapur, made Valerian kneel to the side of the former's horse. The king would use the emperor as a foot stool in order to mount his steed. After Valerian's death, he was skinned and his hide was hung in a Persian temple as a trophy to the triumph of the Persian king over the Roman emperor. This story's veracity is disputed, however, it does give us an idea that Rome was growing ever weaker and had become openly reviled among its neighbors.

His successor, Gallienus (reigned 253-268 CE) would actually rule even longer. He installed his son as co-emperor in the year 260, though his son wouldn't live out the month of his ascension. Problems were still widespread within Rome and without, but it was almost starting to look like the crisis was on its way out. That is, until Gallienus was killed by his own men.

Claudius Gothicus (reigned 268-270 CE) wasn't assassinated, but died of natural causes only a year and some change after his rise to the rank of Caesar. He was succeeded by his brother Quintillus, but the latter wouldn't reign long enough to make it into the histories to any degree farther than his name.

His successor, Aurelian (reigned 270-275 CE) lasted a seemingly healthy five years before being assassinated by the Praetorian Guard.

The next emperor, Tacitus (reigned 275-276 CE,) was the first emperor in a long time to have been elected by the senate itself, rather than simply accepted by it, or having usurped the title. Though he would only live about nine months after becoming Caesar, he did launch a largely successful campaign against the Goths. The reason for his death is speculated, but unknown.

Tacitus's brother, Florian (reigned June-September 276 CE,) would be the next emperor, and the next to be killed by his own men in favor of someone else.

Probus (reigned 276-282 CE,) the fourth to last emperor of the Principate, would reign for six years until he, like so many before him, would be killed by his own men.

Carus (reigned 282-283 CE) was one of the few of this era to die of natural causes, though his rule would only last about ten, maybe eleven months.

The final two emperors of the Principate were Numerian (reigned 283-284 CE) and his brother Carinus (reigned 283-285 CE.) Their deaths are not entirely clear, although it is possible that Carinus fell to the man who would become the first emperor of the Dominate, Diocletian.

As if the civil wars, assassinations, usurpations and general mass power grab weren't bad enough in themselves, Rome still had to be ruled during this period of time. Many of the emperors did what they could, but were simply killed too quickly to make much of an impact. Disease continued to rage for many years through the empire and Rome's enemies were constantly trying to advance. With the beginning of Diocletian, things would take a new turn, this time, changing the nature of the Roman Empire in its entirety.

The Birth of the Dominate and the Partitioning of Rome

Rome was in decline. Years of fighting amongst themselves for rule, or in favor of this or that general or governor had so weakened the power of Rome itself that drastic measures would be imposed in one last-ditch attempt to preserve the role of emperor in Rome.

While the role of the senate was largely ceremonial, only having as much impact as a given Caesar had political blind spots, it had remained a constant from Augustus all the way through to the final emperors of the Principate. With Diocletian (ruled 284-305 CE,) however, this would change. The emperors (I'll explain that in a moment) would hold ultimate power, no longer pretending some sort of shared rule between emperor and senate. The Principate, or rule by emperors installed or accepted by the senate, had ended. The Dominate had begun

Diocletian would construct a new constitution for Rome. Among its provisions was the institution of not only a single emperor, but of two. These were called Augusti (plural of Augustus,) with one ruling over the western part of the empire, including Italy and

Rome itself, while the other would rule over the eastern portion of the empire. From this point onward, the west would spiral into relative powerlessness to the east's prodigious rise to the center of the empire.

These Augusti would have real and ultimate power, without fear of being overruled, as they replaced the authority of the senate with their own authority. Any law or decree sent forth by an Augustus was law of the land, and would remain so in perpetuity unless a future emperor overturned it. This gave the Augusti not only greater control over the immediate future of Rome, but a lasting set of dictates.

The Augusti were not the only rulers, though. Just beneath them were two Caesars, one in the east, one in the west. Thus the highest division of government under Diocletian was called the tetrarchy, or rule by four. Diocletian ruled in the east, near the Persian border and assigned the Caesar Galerius to himself to help with administrative duties and command of the armies. In the west, he had already installed Maximian as Augustus in Rome, but Diocletian actually had Maximian move his place of residence from Rome itself to Milan in order to better handle Germanic incursions. To Maximian, Diocletian assigned the Caesar, Constantius. Rome, though still one empire, had been divided for the sake of administration.

Now, it wasn't uncommon for an emperor to spend much of his rule outside the walls of Rome itself. Under Diocletian, though, it was accepted that the rule over the entire empire was no longer possible by a single man. Trying to hold the empire together, specifically in the west, was becoming more difficult. The Crisis of the Third Century had taken its toll, and military campaigns against the empire had hardly grown less frequent.

Diocletian's rule would see warfare with Persia, but this actually led to Roman victory and annexation of more lands in the east. As there were nearly constant incursions of one army or another in one or more portions of the empire, his tetrarchy had allowed Rome to better tend to the military needs of the empire. Stunningly, though, Diocletian actually severed the connection between politicians and soldiers. That is, outside of his own command and those of the tetrarchy over the armies. These measures helped to ensure not only that the empire was safer from outside attacks, but from mutiny and insurrection within the Roman ranks and citizenry.

This didn't stop warfare with the external world, however, as Diocletian was forced to reclaim Egypt when it declared its independence. The tetrarchy would fight on multiple fronts throughout Diocletian's rule.

Things on the domestic front weren't all wine and cheese, either. It was during Diocletian's rule that the tenth and most extreme persecution of Christians occurred. Though Christianity was to succeed the religion of the Romans in a matter of years, Diocletian issued a number of decrees that would strip Christians of their rights and force them to comply with the state religion of the time. They lost property and were largely discriminated against, though the severity of this persecution would vary depending on the segment of Rome and its primary head of state. All told, a population of between 3,000-3,500 Christians was killed during this final and most severe persecution.

Unlike his predecessors, Diocletian wouldn't die in office or be otherwise removed. He simply abdicated in the year 305 CE. Maximian also abdicated at the same time. While this was likely intended to show that succession to the throne didn't have to come as a result of coup, this action led to yet another civil war.

Civil War, Reunification and the Construction of the Bible under the First Christian Emperor

It was assumed that Constantine and Maxentius, sons of Constantius and Maximian, respectively, would replace Diocletian and Maximian. This didn't happen, rather, Galerius and Constantius were elevated to the role of Augusti with Maximinus and Severus as their Caesars. This began the second tetrarchy, but it wouldn't last long.

Constantius died in 306. The succession to his station would be contested. Galerius, the Augustus, named Severus as the new Augustus in Constantius's place while Constantius's troops named Constantine the new Augustus. Having been left out of the consideration, Maxentius did battle with Severus, deposing him, but failing to claim the title for himself without dispute.

Maxentius, Maximian, Constantine and Galerius all claimed the title of Augustus with only Galerius actually holding the role initially. It's said that, at this point, Galerius met with then-retired Diocletian and Maximian, who claimed to be retired himself, to figure things out. They decided to install a new party, Licinius, as Augustus, making Constantine his Caesar. The role of Galerius as Augustus and Maximinus as Augustus and Caesar, respectively, would not change. As for Maxentius, he was declared a usurper and was thus not considered for a position. This plan backfired.

Licinius's ascent to Augustus was insufferable to both Caesars, each of them seeing themselves as the next in line for the office. Maxentius, with a great deal of support, practically ruled over Africa and Italy itself. Civil war broke out after both Constantine and Maximinus were first given the title of Filius Augusti, or Son of Augustus—a title which basically meant nothing, as the two were already Caesars—and were finally declared Augusti over their parts of the empire.

Thus, there were no longer two Augusti and two Caesars. There were now four Augusti, four full rulers... and they hated each other.

Maximian would eventually commit suicide in the year 310, forced into the act by Constantine. Galerius died, but of natural causes in 311. Constantine finally defeated his foe Maxentius in 312. Maximinus killed himself after suffering a crushing defeat at the hands of Licinius. This would end with Constantine over the empire of the west and Licinius over the empire of the east. The war between the claimants wasn't over, but it would take Constantine eleven years to finally defeat Licinius and claim all of Rome for himself.

During Constantine's reign, he would declare Constantinople, formerly Byzantium and renamed by Constantine after himself, the capitol of the eastern portion of the empire.

Famously, he would also convert to Christianity and decided that Christianity needed one central text, as the Christians of the time varied largely on what they considered to be scripture. After initially declaring himself Christian and legalizing the practice of Christianity, Christians would find themselves in heated debates regarding different doctrines and interpretations of the same. This led to widespread bloodshed among the Christians, one to another. In order to put an end to the slaughter the Christians were levying against each other, Constantine realized that one official doctrine must be adopted. If this didn't happen, the Christians were likely to destroy themselves and undermine Rome and, indeed his rule, in the process. This would be decided by edict of the emperor. The first council of Nicea, the initial meeting which would select what books would become what we now know as the Bible, was held and the centralized text Constantine had hoped for was assembled.

While it's believed by many that Constantine never gave up his pagan beliefs, in order to unify Rome under his rule, the empire would become Christian. The Christian cult in Rome, unlike that of the pagan cults before it, was an ascetic one, preaching discipline and, above all else, a single, all-powerful god. This was a strong political move by Constantine as the religion reflected what he saw as the ideal Rome: That of one all-powerful ruler who tended over an empire of disciplined and self-denying citizens who believed that suffering was an indication of piety.

This wasn't simply accepted by all Romans, however. A man named Julian, later called Julian the Apostate, fought to protect Rome's heritage and its traditional pagan system. He would fall, however, and Christianity within the empire would become the norm. However, pagans weren't the only ones to be disenfranchised. Christians who weren't among the orthodoxy were also supplanted. Rome hadn't only become a Christian empire, but a one-sect Christian empire which dealt harshly with other sects of the religion.

The Death Throes of an Empire

After the death of Constantine in 337 CE, due to pro-
longed illness, he was succeeded by his sons Constantine II, Constantius II and Constans I. They would
rule the empire jointly, but all was not peace. Constantine II was killed, his army battling his brother
Constans I's army.

It would be in the year 360 CE that Julian the Apostate would become emperor. After the death of Constantius II in 361 CE, Julian would be the sole ruler
of all Rome. As mentioned at the end of the previous
section, he is often best known for attempting to return Rome to its pagan roots, but with his death, this
push would end. After the death of Julian the Apostate, Rome would again be split in two, this time by
two brothers, the Augusti Valens and Valentinian.

In the year 364, these brothers became emperors of
Rome and decided to divide the empire into the eastern portion, to be ruled by Valens, the western portion ruled by Valentinian. Rome itself had already
become much less important, and was being thoroughly overshadowed by Constantinople in the east.

The difference between the wealthy and the poor in
Rome was never small, but during the final years of
Rome itself, it grew to a massive income gap. As his-

tory has shown, time and again, this degree of wealth imbalance will end one of two ways: Either in restructuring and at least some level of wealth redistribution or in economic collapse. For Rome, it would be the latter.

The poor would bear the brunt of the economic crisis, being taxed at unprecedented rates while the wealthy largely held onto their vast treasures. While it was necessary for taxation to increase in order for the empire to continue to function, these taxes were largely avoided by the wealthier citizens, their portions often squeezed from the poor. This led to widespread famine and yet further separation between the wealthy and the poor. Not only did this cause the economy of Rome to collapse, it led to widespread unrest and even uprisings.

Rather than simply rectify the situation by ensuring that the rich paid a fair portion of taxes, espionage became commonplace, specifically directed at the poorer members of society. The Roman postal service would become one of the primary sources for information as correspondences were read and used to preempt rebellion.

Christianity had united much of Rome, specifically among the plebeians, but it would not be able to save the Western Empire. In 378 CE, the emperor Valens would meet an army of Goths in battle at Adrianople. This was to be a decisive moment for the empire of the west that had already seen so much hardship, culminating in a great loss of its own power. Though attempting to reclaim Rome's place as the superior military force, Valens and his men were overwhelmed, the army was utterly destroyed and the emperor of the west, dead.

Rome's long held tactic of absorbing the people it conquered into its empire, proclaiming them as Roman citizens, had finally backfired. At this point in time, there were likely as many Germanic soldiers within the Roman Army as there were fighting against it. The Romans, however, continued to think themselves as superior and deny the Germanic peoples the power that the Romans held themselves. With so much of the Western Empire under the influence of the Germanic tribes, both inside and outside of Roman citizenry and service, it would only be a matter of time before Rome succumbed to these vicious warriors.

The Sack of Rome and the End of the Western Empire

When the Goth King, Alaric, settled his people within the bounds of the Roman Empire, he originally wanted only peace and dignity from Rome. The Romans, by this time had become extremely xenophobic, particularly of the Germanic tribes and of the Huns. The barbarians had been largely enslaved within the bounds of the Roman Empire for hundreds of years previous to Alaric's incursion and tensions had only grown over time.

An educated man, fluent in Latin, Alaric sought a position as a general of one of the Rome's armies. Being that he was a Goth, he was denied this post. Although Alaric and his people had only wanted to be a part of Rome, respected and afforded the same opportunities of the Romans, this denial would turn this Goth leader into Rome's greatest threat.

In 410 CE, Alaric led his forces south, intending on forcing the Romans to recognize his people as equals and to afford them the same rights and privileges as the Romans. Rome, by this time, was either wholly incapable or wholly unwilling to fight Alaric's onslaught. Much of the Roman peasantry actually joined the Goths, as their own treatment under Rome had become so abysmal. Alaric would lead his men to sack Rome, but not without once again trying to reason with Rome itself.

With his army now camped outside the gates of Rome, Alaric asked that his people be given a portion of land, measuring approximately 30,000 square miles, in modern day Austria in the Danube River Valley. Rome, ever prideful, refused his demand. Alaric and his men besieged the city, but they held back. When word came from Alaric, he now demanded not only the land, but 5,000 pounds of gold, 30,000 of silver, 4,000 silk tunics, 3,000 skins died scarlet and 3,000 pounds of pepper. In exchange for this, he promised that the Romans would, if nothing else, be spared their lives.

The next turn wouldn't come from the Romans as they were content to postpone any decision on the matter, but from barbarian slaves from within the city. These slaves saw Alaric as a liberator and threw open the gates of Rome, allowing Alaric and his army to enter the city. This once-mighty former seat of the empire was sacked. Rome had fallen. While this wouldn't be the final breath of the Roman Empire, it's fair to say that this was a blow from which the Western Empire simply wouldn't recover.

The various Germanic tribes would not do as the Romans feared and destroy Rome and the former Western Empire. They would simply move and resettle in these lands, stretching throughout the western portion of the once-great empire. In fact, the peoples who the Romans had thought to be so vicious and rapacious simply settled themselves among the Romans, wanting nothing more at this point than peace. They didn't want Rome to crumble; they just wanted to be a part of it.

The sack of Rome in 410 CE is one of a few points traditionally thought to be the fall of the Roman Empire, at least the Western Empire. It is more accurate, however, to place the fall in the year 476 CE.

After Alaric sacked Rome, there was still a succession of distinctly Roman Emperors. These emperors, however, did not wield anything like the power their predecessors had. The reach of the Roman Emperors of the West had already been diminished before the sack of 410 CE, but after this time, the emperors saw what was left of their power evaporate.

Finally, in the year 476 CE, Rome was again attacked by Germanic tribes, this time led by Odoacer. The emperor of the time, ironically, was named Romulus. He had led Rome for less than a year when he was deposed by Odoacer. For the first time, Rome's emperor, the leader of the army that had taken the city and unseated Romulus, was a barbarian.

By this point, the western empire of Rome had already become so weak that it did very little but levy taxes upon its citizenry. Weary of this, rich landowners would begin to fortify their own lands and rule over them by making deals with their barbarian neighbors, thus creating their own fiefdoms. The Middle Ages had begun.

CONCLUSION

The Roman Empire, in the west at least, would never be the same. The Eastern Empire would continue to grow and thrive for another thousand years and, although this was referred to as the Byzantine Empire by outsiders, these citizens would continue to call themselves Romans.

After the fall of Romulus, Rome would still live under the rule of emperors, though foreign and much weaker than those of the Principate and the early Dominate. The idea of Rome, however, would never fall.

Even today, much of our laws and governmental structures in Europe and North America hearken back, at least in part, to successful practices of the Romans. The languages of European descent are largely based in Latin, though there are some exceptions.

The Western Empire which was the seat of power for the ancient world may have fallen, but it wouldn't be the last empire to rule from Rome. The Holy Roman

Empire, would cover most of Italy, all of Germany and parts of France from 800-1806 CE. While Voltaire may have quipped that it was neither holy, nor Roman, nor an Empire, there was something that still drew people toward the governance of Rome.

I hope you have enjoyed learning about this fascinating culture and empire. While I endeavored to include as much as possible, the legacy of Rome is far too vast to reside within a single text. From wars to periods of peace and prosperity, from philosophy to the domination of the known world, Rome was and still is one of the most important parts of the history of our world.

It has been an absolute delight to share with you a glimpse of Rome, from its humble origins to its tragic demise. May your thirst for history continue and lead you to distant shores in the pursuit of knowledge!

A Preview of
Martin R. Phillips'
Latest Book

NORSE MYTHOLOGY

The religion of the Norse or, as they referred to it, Tradition, has captured the minds of many. Though the religion and beliefs of the Vikings are largely out of practice in the world today, the influence of this religion lives on, and in a very profound way.

In the modern day, we see Norse mythos cropping up in movies, television and anime, as well as video games such as Final Fantasy VII, and in comic books. This interest has also reached into the world of music, both from indigenous genres such as the black metal of Norway and other Scandinavian countries, but can be found in various other forms of music and artistic expression.

But what *did* the Norse believe? How did they view the world and what was their conception of their gods? In this book, it is my aim to give you, the reader, an overview of Norse mythology in a way that's not only informative, but interesting.

As with my other texts on mythology (Greek Mythology and Egyptian Mythology) I've found the most effective way to communicate the stories and religion of the Norse is through their stories.

Like many societies, much of Norse lore has been lost to the ages. However, there are a few good sources in this regard, specifically the Eddas. The Poetic Edda in particular is a treasure-trove of insight into the Norse belief system and, through that lens, the Norse way of life.

One thing worthy of mention here is that the central texts still extant on Norse Tradition, namely, the Poetic Edda and the Prose Edda, were written in the thirteenth century. The Tradition, however, was around long before that. As this is the case, much of the knowledge that we now have of the Norse is incomplete and, in some cases, the Poetic Edda disagrees with the Prose Edda. The Poetic Edda, as mentioned above, is particularly insightful, however, as it collects and shares many of the stories of the Norse people.

While this book is not a complete record of the Norse beliefs (and such a record is, to my knowledge, nonexistent,) it has been my pleasure to assemble some of the most pertinent and interesting myths of the Norse. We'll find Odin on his many quests for knowledge and wisdom, the formation of the world out of the body of a giant and we even find Thor in a veiled wedding dress (no, seriously.) From the birth of the sun and moon to the berserkers of Valhalla to the eventual destruction and reformation of the nine worlds, the Norse Tradition tells of captivating gods and goddesses, of heroes and unmitigated disasters.

The pantheon of the Norse is large, like that of the Greeks, Romans and Egyptians. While some principal players such as Odin, Thor and Loki are well-fixed in the popular mindset, many others exist which are just as compelling. The Tradition of the Norse is filled with stories of valor and treachery, love and hatred, Valhalla and Hel. So, from the creation of the cosmos, according to the Norse, all the way through Ragnarök and beyond, I invite you to share this fascinating journey with me into one of the most iconic cultures the world has ever known...

PS. If you enjoyed this book, please help me out by kindly leaving a review!

59907590R00188

Made in the USA
Lexington, KY
19 January 2017